HARLEY DAVIDSON

Dorothea Briel

CHARTWELL
BOOKS, INC.

Special thanks are due for their valuable help in the by no means always easy search for photos and facts for this book to the motorcycle magazine *Motorrad, Reisen & Sport* and its staff, to Herr Klaus Zobel and Manfred Kozlowsky of Harley-Davidson Germany, and to the photographer and Harley-Davidson specialist Albert Saladini.

Picture credits:

Motorrad, Reisen & Sport archive, Cologne: pages 6, 52, 58, 63, 64, 66, 67
Harley-Davidson Germany archive, Mörfelden: pages 10, 12, 13, 15-19, 21-23, 25-27, 30-34, 36-39, 41, 43-57, 59, 64-66, 70-74
Dorothea Briel, Grafschaft: pages 4, 5
Knut Briel, Grafschaft: pages 6, 7, 8, 53
Jürgen Mainx, Bonn: page 9
Frank Ratering, Cologne: pages 4, 8
Albert Saladini, Montpellier: pages 3, 4, 14, 23, 24, 28, 29, 35, 37, 71
Jan Hardy Sommer, Cologne: front cover and pages 8, 60, 67, 68, 69, 70, 71, 74
Wolfgang Spankowski, Reichshof: pages 66, 67
Thomas Zimmerman, Cologne: pages 65, 68, 74

Translated by:
Lilian R. Hall
in association with First Edition Translations Ltd, Cambridge, UK

Published by
CHARTWELL BOOKS, INC.
A Division of **BOOK SALES, INC.**
110 Enterprise Avenue
Secaucus. New Jersey 07094

CLB 4096
© 1994 this English language edition CLB Publishing, Godalming, Surrey
Originally published in German by V.I.P.
© 1992 Paul Zsolnay Verlag Ges.m.b.H, Vienna
All rights reserved
Printed in Italy
ISBN 0-7858-0081-6

The Harley-Davidson legend

Harley-Davidson – the name conjures up all kinds of images: freedom, adventure, endless American highways, *Easy Rider*. Even people who have never sat astride a motorbike in their lives, let alone a Harley-Davidson, know that the name has quite specific associations. Harley-Davidson is not just a make of motorcycle – the images, people and events linked with it have turned it into a legend.

Trying to explain this myth in a few words would be as useless as trying to sell a Japanese motorbike to Willie G. Davidson, the last heir of the firm's founders to be still active in what has become an American institution. At least this is what I took the inscription on a T-shirt to mean that I saw in 1991 at Daytona Beach's 50th Bike Week, one of the annual highlights of the Harley-Davidson community. The T-shirt was on display in a Main Street shop window and read: "Harley-Davidson – if I had to explain, you wouldn't understand."

Nevertheless, I will attempt an explanation. I guess the most promising way to convey the Harley-Davidson legend is to recount the checkered and exciting history of the world's oldest make of motorbike still in production – a history that reaches back almost to the beginning of this century. This book will therefore cover the development of Harley-Davidson motorbikes and the different models produced of a make that is the last to survive out of about 200 former American motorcycle manufacturers.

The words "oldest" and "last" can both still be applied to Harley-Davidson today – although not everyone thinks of the make in terms of superlatives. A Harley-Davidson is by no means the largest,

Unique on the motorcycle scene is the Harley-Davidson riders' sense of community – they feel bound to one another by their on-the-road lifestyle.

Harley-Davidson riders speak the same language, experience the same feelings, are free, equal and united, whether they are at Daytona Beach, Florida, during Bike Week, at their local motorcycle shop, or going for a spin on a Sunday.

4

heaviest, fastest or most powerful motor-bike in the world, as you would be led to believe by its impressive image. Each of these superlatives may have applied to a Harley-Davidson at some time during the history of the motorbike, but since the Japanese manufacturers began outdoing each other over the last twenty or so years, they have produced a bike which is at least on a par with a Harley-Davidson in every category. A Kawasaki VN 15 has a similar V-twin motor to a Harley-Davidson big twin, but with 160cc greater cubic capacity. A Honda Gold Wing is just as luxurious a touring machine as a Harley-Davidson Electra Glide Classic, but even heavier. The fastest speed is no longer a subject for discussion as far as Harley-Davidson is concerned: the 74 F took the 100 mph record before the war, but the fastest superbikes from the Far East are now approaching the 190 mph mark. The power of the 140 hp hypermodern Japanese four-cylinder bikes has long since been limited by laws and agreements instead of by technical feasibility, while the venerable two-cylinder bikes from the USA run out of steam at less than 50 hp because of increasing environmental commitment. No wonder, for the V-twin from Milwaukee, Wisconsin, has been built largely unchanged since

5

1936. Even the record for the most expensive bike is no longer held by the USA. An Italian Bimota Tesi is almost twice as expensive as a Harley-Davidson Tour Glide Ultra Classic, and a Japanese Honda NR 750 is more than three times as expensive. The American motorbikes still belong in the higher price category – you cannot be a Harley-Davidson owner for less than 3,995 dollars, the price of a Sportster 883 – and for the price of a 1,340cc big twin you could buy a stylish medium-sized car. Even so, Harley-Davidson bikes cannot be classed as luxury goods either in the States or abroad, for luxury goods are generally used by a specific social stratum – or have you ever seen a plumber in a Rolls Royce? However, Harley-Davidsons are owned and driven by people of all trades and professions, from all income groups, from all backgrounds, and of all colors and nationalities.

A lawyer may choose to spend part of his tax repayment on a bike, and a laborer may scrimp and save, but they will both end up buying the same model, for the Harley-Davidson range cannot be divided into bikes for the poor and bikes for the rich – they are simply bikes for people with different tastes. And there are plenty of them. Without offering such highly specialized machines as cross-country enduros and speedway superbikes, the Harley-Davidson range only comprises two different engines and three series, but there are a total of more than 20 models. No other motorcycle manufacturer offers a larger range, and none makes such clever use of the unit construction system, thus ensuring a problem-free supply of spare parts and straightforward servicing. All this adds up to there being Harley-Davidson bikes for almost all ambitions and tastes, and the entire range of possibilities is exploited by the customers. On a Harley-Davidson the differences between worker and academic become blurred. The only obvious things are the rider's preference for a chopper or full dresser, for cruising or touring, and a common liking for a technical concept that may be outdated, but gives one the feeling of owning a piece of technology that has become a legend.

Within the large Harley-Davidson family, anyone can give full expression to his or her individualistic tendencies, but its members ultimately feel as though they belong together. This applies particularly when motorcycling is going through a difficult period, such as immediately after the war, when the factory was only producing two models, and it remained up to the Harley-Davidson owner and his technical skills to give the bike a personal touch. In those days, Harley-Davidson owners would almost inevitably hug each other on meeting. Today, they would probably content themselves with a handshake, such as they would not offer to the rider of another make of bike, but their solidarity is undiminished. A Harley-Davidson rider would never dissociate

On a Harley-Davidson, more than on any other motorcycle, the differences between worker and academic become blurred.

The only obvious things are the rider's preference for a chopper or dresser, and a common liking for a technical concept that gives one the feeling of owning a piece of technology that has become a legend.

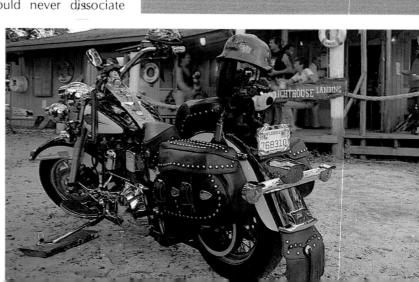

himself from another – unless perhaps the other were a member of an organized gang who classed himself among the one per cent of outlaw bikers.

This feeling of belonging together among Harley-Davidson riders is based at least in part on the distinctiveness of these Wisconsin motorbikes. If you were to remove the trademark from a number of Japanese motorbikes, only an expert would be able to tell a Honda from a Kawasaki or ā Yamaha from a Suzuki. However, a child can recognize a Harley-Davidson at first glance, no matter what the model. It does not matter either whether the bike was built in 1936 or 1992, for the V-twin engine has undergone little external change over almost six decades, and the style of the Milwaukee designer has remained unmistakable for just as long. Undeterred by fashion trends, but inspired by ideas from dealers and customers alike, the Harley-Davidson company has continued to build on the existing design.

There is something even more important which contributes to the feeling of belonging together: in spite of all the differences between people who ride Harley-Davidsons, and for all their individualism, they know that they agree on a fundamental attitude that is characterized by a striving for freedom and a sense of justice, and at times even by an intolerance of those who think and feel differently, and which is often compared to the *joie de vivre* of the former American cowboy. Perhaps one can even say that these people have a common way of life. To be sure, the doctor has a different home life from that of the construction worker, but on the road they are free, equal and united on their machines – as long as they both ride the "right" bike.

Harley-Davidson riders speak the same language and experience the same feelings, no matter where they are: at Daytona Beach, Florida, during Bike Week; at the Black Hill Motorcycle Classic in Sturgis, South Dakota, where tens of thousands of Harley-Davidson riders converge annually; at their local Harley-Davidson shop, purchasing spares; or at a chance meeting during a Saturday evening spin.

Klaus Zobel, manager of the German branch of the Harley-Davidson Motor Company, projects this phenomenon entirely onto the motorbikes: "We sell people a philosophy of life and throw in

a motorbike for free." Even though he says this with a twinkle in his eye, there is something to it: these motorbikes not only bring together the same type of people, who share the same fundamental attitude, but these people's feelings towards their bikes go far beyond loyalty to a particular marque. Couples get married on their Harley-Davidsons, the bike is allowed to spend the winter in the living room, men and women wear the logo on their shirts, jackets and ties, or even have it tattooed on their bodies.

The company laid the foundation for this close relationship in the 1930s, when dealers and customers were made aware of the rigorous demarcation between Harley-Davidson and Indian, the second-ranking American motorbike company which was still in existence at that time. This was part of a policy of competition for business aimed at insuring survival in the collapsing motorcycle market of the Depression. As we know today, this strategy continued to be successful at every stage in the company's history. Not only do Harley-Davidson riders not like other makes of motorbike, they do not know and will not accept any other make than their own, and despise Japanese motorbikes as "rice cookers."

Even in better times, the company made a point of fostering close links between employees, dealers, customers and the name of Harley-Davidson – again with success. Most people who work in the Harley-Davidson factories in Milwaukee, Wisconsin, and York, Pennsylvania, or who work for an authorized dealer, like, ride and live Harley-Davidson. Second or third generation employees who have been working for Harley-Davidson for twenty years or more are not unusual. The longest-serving employee was an office worker in Milwaukee who

The Harley-Davidson company has always promoted a healthy American patriotism, which has become synonymous with the marque.

Not for nothing does the star-spangled banner so often adorn Harley-Davidsons. The eagle, both the heraldic bird of the USA and the Harley-Davidson trademark, is a universal symbol of the longing for limitless freedom.

finally retired after 64 years of service. Customers' requirements are taken care of by a whole package of measures, from factory tours and test ride promotions, from the house journal *The Enthusiast* and membership of the Harley-Davidson Owners Group HOG, to charity runs and meetings supported or even organized by the company. This is a "Close to the Customer Policy" at its best.

Finally, Harley-Davidson has always promoted a healthy American patriotism, which has also become synonymous with the marque. Not for nothing does the star-spangled banner adorn some models. The eagle, both the heraldic bird of the USA and the Harley-Davidson trade mark, symbolizes the American biker's loyalty to his country and to the old pioneering spirit. For Harley-Davidson fans overseas it symbolizes a

longing for the limitless freedom which the country of unlimited opportunities still holds out to motorbike riders at least.
Is this all too much emotion surrounding an inanimate object? Film star Mickey Rourke doesn't think so, and no doubt thousands of other Harley-Davidson fans would agree: "It's a personal thing that can't be described. It's part of you."

1901
US president McKinley is assassinated, his successor is the former vice president Theodore "Teddy" Roosevelt. In the USA, Gustave Whitehead succeeds in making the first powered flight.

1902
Robert Bosch invents the spark plug. Enrico Caruso makes his first phonograph recording.

1903
The Dutchman Willem Einthoven invents the electrocardiograph. In the USA, Edwin S. Porter films the first Western *The Great Train Robbery*.

1904
Great Britain and France enter into an *Entente Cordiale*. The Russo-Japanese war breaks out.

1905
The first revolution in Tsarist Russia fails. Anna Pavlova dances the *Dying Swan* for the first time.

1906
Norwegian Roald Amundsen navigates the Northwest Passage. In San Francisco, over 500 people die in an earthquake and the subsequent fire which rages for three days.

1907
Depression in the USA. American Ann Jarvis starts off the tradition of Mother's Day.

1908
Henry Ford's Model T is launched in Detroit. In Britain, Robert Baden-Powell founds the first Scout group.

1901-1908

The early days and the "Silent Gray Fellow" single

The history of Harley-Davidson begins in the year 1901 with a fairly basic but exciting idea thought up by Americans William "Bill" Harley and Arthur Davidson. The two friends, who had been inseparable companions since childhood and who both worked in the same factory in Milwaukee, Wisconsin – Harley as a draftsman and Davidson as a pattern maker – wanted to take the hard work out of cycling with the aid of an internal-combustion engine.

The idea was by no means new. The E.R. Thomas company was already building motorized bicycles at that time. And the two young men, one 21, the other 20, did not have a sense of mission with regard to motorcycles in those days either. Like many of their contemporaries, they were merely enthusiastic amateur designers who were always trying out new ideas and wanted to find a practical use for their designs. The pair took it into their heads to

The first Harley-Davidson from 1903. A total of three were built that year; the first motorcycle sold completed 100,000 miles in ten years.

construct an internal-combustion engine. Initially, they considered the most useful application for such an engine to be as a means of propulsion for a boat. Bill Harley was a keen angler, and his friend Arthur Davidson sometimes went rowing with him on one of the many lakes around Milwaukee.

Once bitten by the idea, the two friends proceeded to read the technical journals which at that time were proliferating like mushrooms. They came across articles on the motorization of the bicycle so often that they finally decided to fix their future engine onto a bicycle instead of a boat. After all, Bill Harley had trained in a bicycle factory. The two men realized that there was a lot of research and development still to be done in connection with the motorization of the bicycle. They were thrilled by the well-nigh inexhaustible possibilities which this area offered to their creative

urge – even if most of their fellow human beings dismissed their ideas and plans with a shrug of the shoulders.

Harley and Davidson began to be taken more seriously when they joined forces with another draftsman from their company, a German by the name of Emil Kröger, who had recently settled in the USA. Kröger had previously worked for Aster in Paris and had brought with him the latest drawings for the De Dion

11

gasoline engine. The German's specialist knowledge, Harley's experience in building bicycles and Davidson's models of small gasoline engines, based on Kröger's blueprints, gave the three of them the courage to open a workshop. However, financial resources and tools for equipping their workshop were in extremely short supply and they still did not have a good mechanic.

The problem of a mechanic solved itself when Davidson's brother Walter, a railroad machinist in Parson, Kansas, came to Wisconsin for the wedding of the third Davidson brother, William, and became so enthusiastic about the idea of building a motorcycle that he immediately stayed on in Wisconsin.

From then on, Bill Harley, the two Davidson brothers and their German friend spent every spare minute in their workshop. Since they did not own a lathe, they had to keep going over to an acquaintance's workshop, to whom they promised an engine housing as payment when their first engine was finished.

Evenings and weekends were spent making engine parts by hand, and gradually the first Harley-Davidson engine took shape. In addition to what they learnt from the De Dion blueprints, the four men were able to glean information from the motorcycles that were already on the market. Among the companies producing them were such famous names as Indian, Marsh, Orient, Pope, Thor and Wagner, but there were also many fly-by-night companies founded by people who hoped to make a fast buck manufacturing motorcycles and who quickly gave up when things went wrong.

In order to understand today the extent of the problems that confronted the Harley-Davidson pioneers, it is necessary to recall the stage technological development had reached at the beginning of the century. There were virtually no reliable manuals on engine technology. Ready-made parts were in extremely short supply, so almost every single engine part had to be made by hand. If we are to believe the stories that were handed down, the first Harley-Davidson carburetor was made from a tomato can, and the first spark plug turned out to be as large as a doorknob. When it was finally finished, the first engine had a 25 cubic in (400cc) displacement and developed a maximum of 3 hp. The back wheel was driven directly – without a clutch or gears – via a flat leather belt.

Tests soon showed that this first engine was too weak to have any practical use. It was only able to drive the bicycle onto which it was built along an absolutely level road at a speed of 25 mph. The slightest incline meant that the rider had to pedal in order to keep going. Also, the bicycle was not able to take the strain, and the frame and forks soon broke. Harley and the Davidsons had to go back to the drawing board. They more than doubled the diameter of the engine's flywheel, and designed a single-loop frame which replaced the diamond bicycle frame of the first model. Although the three spent every spare minute working on their motorcycle, it took several months before they had even developed a suitable carburetor. In this they were greatly helped by a certain Ole Evinrude, who was later to make his name with outboard motors. By 1903, Harley and the Davidsons had the problems

under control and were ready to put their first motorcycle into production.

The year 1903 was an outstanding year for motorization in America. Harley and the Davidsons brought out their first motorcycle, and Henry Ford founded his Ford Motor Company, which presented the Model T to the public five years later. The brothers Orville and Wilbur Wright also designed and flew the first powered aircraft.

The motorcycle pioneers' rented workshop soon became too small, and the three of them needed something larger of their own. With the help of Davidson senior, a carpenter by trade, they built their own workshop in the Davidsons' back yard on 38th Street, on the corner of Highland Avenue, and painted "Harley-Davidson Motor Co." on the door. Their dream had become reality, and the first Harley-Davidson factory opened its doors. The factory building only consisted of a small wooden hut measuring ten by fifteen feet, but it was nonetheless their first very own workshop.

Their first year's production was equally modest: a total of three machines left the new motorcycle factory in 1903, and were already sold and paid for before they were finished. The buyer of the first machine, a Mr. Meyer, traveled 6000 miles on the motorcycle before he sold it to a Mr. Lyon, who rode it for a further 15,000 miles. This first Harley-Davidson changed hands three more times, and in 1913 the factory was able to claim as a selling point that their first production motorcycle had done 100,000 miles, and that the motor was still running on its original bearings after ten years. Reliability was to prove the most important feature of Harley-Davidson motorcycles in years to come.

Another of the first model's features was the machine's relatively low noise by the standards of the time. And since its builders also wanted the publicity to

The founders of Harley-Davidson Motor Company Inc.:
(from left to right)
William A. Davidson,
Walter Davidson,
Arthur Davidson and
William S. Harley.

convey a human side to their motorcycle, which was painted entirely in gray, they gave it the nickname "Silent Gray Fellow." One year on, the company doubled its modest production area, and during 1904 eight motorcycles left the little factory. Over the following year capacity and production again doubled. The first employee was taken on, while Harley and the Davidsons still kept their own jobs, although these were now all but sidelines. The old building was bursting at the seams, and early the next year a new factory was built one block further down on 27th Street, on the corner of Chestnut Street, next to the Chicago, Milwaukee & St. Paul Railroad Company. Once again, this was only a wooden building but, with 2,100 square feet of floor space spread over two stories, it was of considerable size. Chestnut Street was later renamed Juneau Avenue, and the Harley-Davidson head office is still there today.

When the shell of the new factory had been erected, the Davidsons realized that the framework encroached by a few inches upon the neighboring plot of land, which belonged to the railroad company. They solved the problem pragmatically by summoning their friends who just lifted up the entire framework and moved it a little to one side.

The first Harley-Davidson factory: production began in 1903 in a 10x15 ft wooden shed (above). The "factory" area was doubled the following year (left).

The new building cost a great deal, but the Davidsons, who were of Scottish origin and careful with their money, did not want to borrow the necessary capital from a bank. Instead, they borrowed the money from an uncle on their mother's side from Madison, Wisconsin, by the name of James McLay, who had accumulated a degree of wealth through land speculation. Everyone called him the "honey uncle," because his hobby was bee-keeping.

Production in the new factory jumped to 50 motorcycles in 1906, and these were all sold in the Milwaukee area. It began to be time for Harley, whose family came from England, and the Scottish Davidsons to think about finding customers farther afield than Wisconsin if their company's rapid growth was to continue. The three also realized that a proper service network would be needed in future. Such a network would not be easy to develop, since at the time motorcycles were mostly

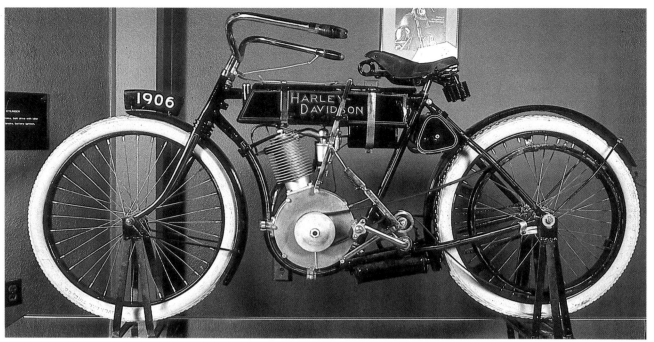

sold by bicycle dealers, and such tradesmen were soon out of their depth as the technology advanced and their workshops became overstretched.

The "Silent Gray Fellow" underwent continuous improvement, and in 1906 it was given a Springer front fork, a form of front wheel suspension thought up by Bill Harley, which was to prove a reliable solution for decades. At that time, most motorcycles had no suspension at all, while streets did not have a tarred surface and were in poor condition. Motorcycles were therefore not a particularly comfortable means of transport, especially since the seat was still nothing more than a bicycle saddle. The unsprung frames were naturally subject to extreme stresses, so that broken frames and forks were almost an everyday occurrence in machines with no suspension.

The first sprung front forks were unable to solve this problem completely, since new difficulties were caused by the lack of damping and the constantly changing wheelbase. With his Springer fork, William Harley produced a design that combined stability, sufficient spring travel and a constant wheelbase. The "Silent Gray Fellow" was enthusiastically received by an increasing number of customers who liked what it had to offer. They liked its comparatively modern design, with an engine that was mounted low down on the stable frame to give a low centre of gravity, and that offered

potential for adjustment via the carburetor and timing. They also liked the belt drive that acted as a clutch: when slack, the leather belt, which connected the crankshaft to the rear wheel, slipped as the crankshaft turned, and the motorcycle remained stationary even though the engine was running; when the rider wanted to move off, he operated a lever to tension the belt and establish the connection between the driving parts. The care with which materials had been chosen and the proportions worked out right from the early days also convinced motorcyclists that this was the machine for them.

Business was now going so well that Bill Harley and the two Davidson brothers gave up their jobs one after the other in order to devote themselves entirely to motorcycle manufacturing. They also took on five more people. However, the three founding members still worked more than an eight-hour day and seldom left the factory before ten o'clock at night. Their families thought themselves lucky when their menfolk came home at eight o'clock on Christmas Eve.

There was nothing more that could hold the company back from being a very big success except the limited technical knowledge of Harley and the Davidsons, none of whom had trained as an engineer. They realized that in-depth knowledge was vital if the company was to continue making progress, so they

decided that one of them would acquire this knowledge through academic study. The student was to be Bill Harley, who left the Davidsons temporarily in charge of the company and began a course of study at the University of Wisconsin in Madison. His main subject was engineering science and, with a view to the company's requirements, he studied internal-combustion engines as his special subject. Harley paid his way as a student by working as a waiter in a fraternity house.

By 1907 the firm had already grown to such an extent that the proprietors incorporated the partnership as a company under state law. On September 22 "Harley-Davidson Motor Company Incorporated" was entered in the company register of the State of Wisconsin. Walter Davidson became president of the company, William Harley's role was as chief engineer and treasurer, and Arthur Davidson became general sales manager and company secretary. In order to get production better under control, the three asked William Davidson, who at 36 was the eldest of the Davidson brothers, to join their company as vice president and works manager. William leapt at the chance, and proved to be very important for the young company with his toolmaker's in-depth knowledge of metalworking. His experience as a former repair workshop foreman with the Chicago, Milwaukee &

In 1908, William Harley began developing the first two-cylinder engine, while the factory premises continued to grow.

In 1907, after just five years, the steadily increasing staff of the Harley-Davidson Motor Company produced 150 motorcycles.

St. Paul Railroad also proved very useful. However, William Davidson was not especially knowledgeable about motorcycles and, strangely, as the only one of the four not to be born in the USA (he was born in Aberdeen), he was never to ride one himself.

Each of the four had an important title, but their areas of authority and tasks were not as clear cut as this would suggest, and each had to step in wherever needed. The president's desk continued for a long time to resemble a workbench, covered as it was with half-finished wheel hubs, shafts, bearings and pistons.

The firm's rapid growth soon meant that new production methods and techniques were required. Each time one of the bosses would do the learning, then pass his knowledge on to the employees. For example, William and Walter Davidson went to Chicago for a short time to learn oxyacetylene welding, then they showed the others what was involved.

Arthur Davidson was now trying to find dealers who would be prepared to sell motorcycles on a franchise basis – that is as independent entrepreneurs – but in the name of Harley-Davidson. He had to try and improve the Harley-Davidson dealer network with good ideas and intensive dealer training in order to make up for the company being slower off the mark than their competitors. For those motorcycle manufacturers who had started off making just bicycles already had a functioning dealer network which

they could expand to receive the new machines. In order to win reputable bicycle dealers over to their side, and also to attract more motorcycle customers by way of the bicycle, Arthur Davidson even started up a bicycle marketing department. Since the capacity in Milwaukee was fully taken up with motorcycle production, Harley-Davidson had the bicycles made by Butler Brothers in Chicago, and then badged them with the company logo before distributing them through their own dealer network. The untiring work put into the company was not without its rewards: a total of 150 motorcycles had been produced by the end of 1907, and some had even been sold to the police. Future prospects looked pretty good, even though many companies were now producing and selling automobiles. However, cars did not present a real threat to the motorcycle industry, but rather served to stimulate demand. They awoke a desire for motorized transport in sectors of the population who could not afford a car and who therefore made do instead with a cheaper motorcycle.

In 1907, the first Harley-Davidson advertising brochure appeared. Until then, occasional advertisements and word of mouth had sufficed to sell all the motorcycles they had produced, but with increasing competition in the USA and rising annual production, professional advertising became indispensable. Once again, the Davidsons went about this in a typically Scottish manner, being careful to the point of parsimony. The advertising agency with which they had an agreement did not receive a fixed annual budget, but was paid order by order after the work had been carried out. The company was to keep to this method, which was unusual in this line of business, for the next 50 years, even for the preparation of complete catalogues and dealer aids.

In 1908 Harley completed his degree in Madison and returned to Milwaukee, to begin immediately by designing a new engine. The single-cylinder Silent Gray Fellow now presented few possibilities for further development, and Harley was looking for a new challenge. Since it first appeared, the single's displacement had been increased by 10 cubic inches (160cc) to 35 cubic inches (575cc), it developed a maximum of 4 hp, did 100 miles to

1.5 gallons of gasoline, and enabled the motorcycle to reach a top speed of 45 mph.

In order to put the reliability of the single to the test, Walter Davidson decided to take part in the New York state endurance run in June 1908. From among the 61 entrants in the two-day event, he was the only Harley-Davidson rider and certainly not one of the favorites. On the second day, only 46 riders remained on the 180-mile circuit around Long Island to Brooklyn, and Walter surprised everyone by winning the race. Just one week later he also won an economy competition staged by the FAM, the Federation of American Motorcyclists.

The Silent Gray Fellow's single-cylinder engine still worked with an atmospheric inlet valve and from this point of view presented opportunities for development, but because of the single's proven performance, Bill Harley concentrated on a much larger project – the development of a two-cylinder engine.

A new motorcycle was therefore urgently needed, since Harley-Davidson was pretty much alone on the American market in having a strategy of only offering a single model. There were now countless manufacturers offering a whole range of models and the market had become immense. What's more, there were still relatively few companies who manufactured engines and other components, but there were any number of firms who bought in the parts and assembled motorcycles, some of them of doubtful quality, then painted their company logo on the gas tank. In contrast, almost six years after starting production, Harley-Davidson was only just getting around to developing a second model: a motorcycle with a V-twin engine. This basic design was to remain the trademark of the Milwaukee machines for all time.

Prototypes with different cubic capacities were already being tested in 1908 and were presented to the public. For example, *The Bicycling World and Motorcycle Review* was already describing a 53 cubic inch (870cc) Harley-Davidson V-twin machine in its edition of April 25, 1908. In July of the same year, Harvey Bernard won the Hillclimb at Algonquin, Illinois on a Harley-Davidson with a 61 cubic inch (1000cc) V-twin engine. However, the first two-cylinder motorcycles did not reach the sales rooms until February 1909.

Walter Davidson, the company's first president, after his astonishing victory in the New York state endurance run in 1908.

By 1908 horse-drawn carts were a thing of the past at Harley-Davidson. The first trucks, made by Brush, were put into service.

1909
William Howard Taft is elected 27th president of the USA. American Robert Edwin Peary is the first person to reach the North Pole.

1910
In Mexico, revolution breaks out against the dictator Porfirio Diaz.

1911
The first transcontinental flight by powered airplane across the USA takes 82 hours 4 minutes – plus refueling stops.

1912
Woodrow Wilson is the first Democratic candidate to win the presidential elections since 1896. The *Titanic* sinks following a collision with an iceberg; more than 1500 people drown.

1913
The Panama Canal is finished. Charlie Chaplin makes his first film.

1914
Ford raises the basic worker's wage from $2.40 for a nine-hour day to $5.00 for an eight-hour day. The First World War breaks out in Europe.

1915
Alexander Graham Bell makes the first transcontinental telephone call from New York to San Francisco. Albert Einstein attracts interest with his *General Theory of Relativity*.

1916
Automobile production in the USA exceeds one million, the average price of a car is 600 dollars. US troops march into the Dominican Republic.

1917
The USA enters the First World War and sends troops to France. Congress ratifies Prohibition.

1918
The First World War comes to an end. At this time, more than one million American soldiers are stationed in Europe. The first regular airmail service starts between New York and Washington.

1909-1918

The big twin and the First World War

The year 1909 brought a decisive technical innovation for Harley-Davidson: the two-cylinder engine. The V-twin was based on the single and was equipped with cylinders from the 1908 model but with a slightly smaller bore, giving it a cubic capacity of 1000cc. It developed 7 hp and achieved a speed of 60 mph.

1909 was a successful year for the company: 35 employees produced 1000 motorcycles, the production area was doubled, for the first time using a brick building and not just a wooden construction. At last the company had what could be called a factory, with 5,400 square feet of floor space. At Harley-Davidson they were getting used to being successful; only one year later 149 employees were working in the factory, and between 1909 and 1917 the production area doubled each year.

However, 1909 was also a year of failure, for the new V-twin was not well received by dealers and customers. The atmospherically controlled inlet valve, also known as a snifting valve, had always worked well in the single-cylinder machines, but proved to be unsuitable for two-cylinder motorcycles, and for this reason only a few dozen were built. In 1910, production was halted and Bill Harley set about thoroughly revising the V-twin.

In the new engine, the inlet valve was controlled mechanically in the same way as the exhaust valve. Since the inlet valve remained in its place above the cylinder head, while the exhaust valve was positioned on the side next to the cylinder, this principle was called ioe (inlet over exhaust).

Harley was correct in recognizing that the problems would be solved by controlling the inlet valve mechanically and, when the V-twin was relaunched in 1911,

During 1909, 35 workers produced just over 1000 motorcycles at the Juneau Avenue factory. There was as yet no assembly line, but there were already specialized departments such as the lathe shop (left), the polishing shop (below left) and final assembly (facing page).

the single-cylinder machines were also fitted with this valve control system. The two-cylinder motorcycle also came with a new frame, giving a lower sitting position without losing road clearance, and the purchaser could choose between magneto and battery ignition. Also, Harley-Davidson was now using high tensile steels such as chromium vanadium nickel steel to insure higher tensile strength and maintain the image of reliability.

The patented idler or primitive clutch, which Bill Harley developed in conjunction with his colleague Henry Melk, represented a very important innovation. It was located in the rear wheel and could be operated either by a hand lever or a foot pedal. At last it was possible to interrupt and reinstate the drive between engine and rear wheel when stopping and starting. This meant that the belt drive mechanism already described had become redundant, and the customer could even request power transmission via a roller chain instead of the usual leather belt, which was fairly unreliable and slipped easily in wet conditions.

Last but not least, Harley-Davidsons were now fitted with a sprung saddle. The saddle itself had a good inch of travel thanks to spiral springs attached to the seat bracket. In addition, the seat tube, which could move within the frame downtube, was supported by two progressively wound, 14 inch springs with a total travel of four inches. This must have contributed significantly to the comfort of the ride on bad roads on a motorcycle with a rigidly mounted rear wheel.

In the days when Harley-Davidson's V-twin, simply named the 61 after its cubic capacity, was selling well despite its bad start, motorcycle racing had already become a popular sport. The entertainment value of these events was enormous – there were very few cinemas and as yet neither radio nor television – and a number of local and regional championships had even come into being. Although Walter Davidson had taken part early on in competitions, riding his company's motorcycles, it was the factory's policy not to build any special racing machines and it did not employ a works team. In the *Motorcycle Illustrated* of September 21, 1911, the company declared that it was not concerned with racing, but that if

Harley-Davidson owners won races with their standard machines, it could not help but be triumphant with them. The policy of leaving racing to private riders seemed to pay off: in 1912, the Bakersfield and San Jose races were won by privately-owned, entirely standard Harley-Davidson V-twin machines – in San Jose the motorcycle in second place lagged behind by some 17 miles!

However, keen sportsmen did not exactly welcome the factory's abstinent attitude. Successful sports riders resented the fact that they received no support, even though they contributed so much to the marque's reputation. For the present, there were still Harley-Davidson dealers who would tune motorcycles and support a particular rider, because they realized that racing successes were a good advertisement. In 1913, such machines took the first three places in the 225-mile race from Harrisburg to Philadelphia and back. Curley Fredericks, one such Harley-Davidson rider with a dealer's backing, astounded the crowds when he outdistanced Floyd Clymer on an Excelsior and Steven Boyd on an Indian by a quarter of a mile in a challenge race.

The successes of the Harley-Davidson motorcycles, the popularity of races, which were always attended by large crowds of spectators, and the annoyance of the dealers and sports riders finally led to heated discussions between the members of the firm's management. Then, in mid 1913, Harley-Davidson declared its intention to enter its own riders in races. This decision led Bill Harley to take on an assistant. Although an outstanding engineer constantly anxious to refine and improve, he was no genius at research and development and certainly no inventor – at least this is what his contemporaries imply. After all, the Harley-Davidson ioe engines were still based largely on the European De Dion engine. Harley contacted Bill Ottaway, who was working as chief design and development engineer in the motorcycle department of a large engineering firm, The Aurora Automatic Machine Company. Ottaway had a natural talent for motorcycle technology and was renowned for his revolutionary ideas. Harley managed to lure him away from Aurora, although he made it a condition that he base his development

work at Harley-Davidson on the existing technology instead of developing entirely new designs, which would of course require considerable investment.

In Milwaukee, Bill Ottaway immediately began by overhauling the 61. He succeeded in considerably reducing the vibrations and refining the engine to give smoother and better performance despite the design's inherent defects. Meanwhile, Bill Harley was concentrating on optimizing the power transmission. The direct drive of the early days had become outdated; a transmission was needed, especially for racing applications and for the increasing number of motorcycles with sidecars. The result of his efforts was a two-speed transmission which, together with the primitive clutch already developed by him, was located in the rear wheel. Harley and Ottaway collaborated in the design of the first Harley-Davidson racing version, the long-awaited model IIK. This motorcycle was an immediate success: in the same year Harley-Davidson won the One-Hour National Championship in Birmingham, Alabama, and there were a total of 26 wins in the following year.

While Harley and Ottaway were busy on their development, Arthur Davidson was hard at work improving sales. He visited the dealers and discussed with them the details of model policy and selling points. To maintain close contact between the company and the dealers, he published a magazine entitled *The Dealer*. This gave tips on selling and drew comparisons between Harley-Davidson and other motorcycle marques. Meanwhile, the motorcycle market was growing steadily: in 1913 a total of 71,000 machines was built, the clear market leader being Indian with 31,000 units. Excelsior was at number two, and Harley-Davidson completed the "Big Three" of the motorcycle industry. Cars were still considerably more expensive than motorcycles in the USA: Ford's Model T cost 850 dollars, almost three times the cost of a motorcycle. Also, the first sidecars were now on the market, and these considerably increased the transport capability of the motorcycle. For an additional price of 75 dollars you could transport the whole family. Sidecars were also of interest to business people, since they could be fitted with different superstructures, depending on

From 1913 onwards, Harley-Davidson entered official factory racing machines in the dirt-track races (above), which were extremely popular in the USA. Leslie "Red" Parkhurst (left) was the star of the works team – he snapped up victories and world records until the early 'twenties.

what was required. Harley-Davidson did not have enough space to manufacture sidecars, so bought them from the Riger Company in Chicago. In 1914 Harley-Davidson sold 2,500 sidecars, and as many as 8,500 in 1915.

An important business decision was taken in 1913: Harley-Davidson was now well enough established to start exporting. The first branch outside America was opened in London by the Scot Duncan

When the First World War broke out in 1914, Harley-Davidson had two basic models in its range: the latest version of the single (left), which had been given a 575cc ioe engine in 1911, and the 1000cc V-twin (facing page top), which had been introduced in 1909 and had also been given an ioe engine in 1911.

Watson. The first motorcycles arrived in April 1914 and, when the First World War broke out in August, 350 Harley-Davidsons had already reached the British Isles. The single-cylinder version was not very popular in Britain, but the Europeans were enthusiastic about the V-twin.

Technical refinement of the standard motorcycles continued. For example, the 1915 models were finally given a step-starter. Until then, motorcycles had to be started by pedalling or pushing. The doubly effective drum brake on the rear wheel was also new. From inside, expanding brake shoes pressed against the drum, while pressure was exerted from outside by a tautened brake band. This brake system was the factory's own development, and considerably more expensive than the brake which had previously been bought in. A year later, the step-starter had already been replaced by an improved version, whose mechanism was housed in the gearbox. It was called a kick-starter to differentiate it from the earlier system. A three-speed transmission, a clutch situated on the engine and an improved oil pump were also introduced. Finally, both singles and twins were fitted with a complete electrical system which Harley-Davidson bought in from the Remy group.

There were also innovations in the sales department: *The Dealer* magazine was replaced by *The Enthusiast*, which was published at irregular intervals, also under the direction of the factory. This publication was posted not only to dealers but also to Harley-Davidson owners, and today it can claim to be the longest-running motorcycle magazine in the USA. In addition, Arthur Davidson announced a reorganization of the dealer network in the fall of 1916. The USA was divided up into geographical areas and a factory representative was allocated to each. He was responsible for the dealers in his area and reported directly to Milwaukee. All this was intended to improve contact with dealers, but critics of the new system saw in the factory representatives a monitoring body of Arthur Davidson's, of whom it was said that he kept things on a tight rein.

However, a policy of strict control was apparently necessary, since the repercussions of the world war raging in Europe were starting to affect the American motorcycle market. The supply of many parts such as bearings, magnets and rubber components from the Old World was interrupted.

Also, the inevitable inflationary effects of war caused the prices of many components and materials such as steel, electrical units and tires to rocket. Buyers, whose income lagged behind the level of inflation, failed to materialize. Even in 1915, only 60,000 motorcycles were sold compared with the previous year's 71,000, and the trend continued downwards.

Apart from falling demand, rising wages in automobile manufacturing presented a further problem for the American motorcycle industry. Henry Ford, who employed thousands of workers on his assembly lines, increased the basic wage of 2.40 dollars for a nine-hour day – for years the US standard for industrial workers – to 5.00 dollars for an eight-hour day. Ford was able to do this because of his company's enormously rapid growth and greatly rationalized production methods. He was also convinced that this wage increase would pay off in the long term since well-paid workers would be able to afford a car. Other companies were also forced to increase their wages, and this led to many smaller companies going under. However, despite the difficult economic conditions, Harley-Davidson remained in the black. Contributing factors in this were the cautious development, criticized by some as being too slow, of the company and its products, the conservative company management and, last but not least, the successful involvement in racing. Even the export side flourished despite, or even because of, the war in Europe. British civilian motorcycle production had ceased, and the interest of the British in American motorcycles had been awakened. This helped the reputation of Harley-Davidson machines to spread into Europe where, as already mentioned, the V-twins were especially popular. At this time, American buyers were also changing their allegiances from singles to two-cylinder machines. From now on, singles were mainly used for

Numerous technical innovations date from 1915 and 1916: the step-starter, a new rear-wheel brake, a new clutch and three-speed transmission were introduced, and a three-wheeler version of the V-twin (left) was offered as a delivery and messenger vehicle.

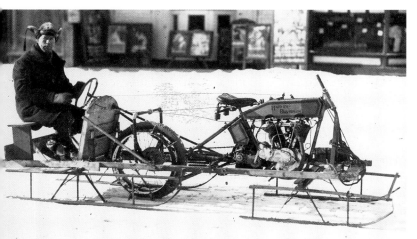

Harley-Davidson riders had a strong tendency towards individuality even in the early days – this is an early snowmobile from 1917 based on the V-twin.

business purposes and in the civil service as transport for messengers and delivery boys.

Harley-Davidson realized sooner than other companies that motor vehicles were going to be needed for waging a modern war, and started building military motorcycles for the army. The USA was not as yet involved in the world war, and President Wilson made the neutrality of the USA in the European conflict into an election issue. However, in 1916 the American army became drawn into military clashes with the Mexican revolutionary Francesco "Pancho" Villa. Villa was incensed that the USA was supporting the Mexican government then in office and took revenge by looting US territory along the Mexican-American border. Harley-Davidson therefore made its first military appearance in Mexico, when a US unit of shock troops under General "Black Jack" Pershing went into battle against the revolutionary. The expedition was not able to wipe out Villa's troops, but it represented the first deployment of motorized US units.

Attacks by the German fleet on American ships were on the increase and

President Wilson, following his reelection, was given authority by Congress to announce mobilization. The USA entered the First World War in 1917, and the same year the Harley-Davidson Service School was founded. The school served primarily as a training center for the armed forces, but also attracted civil mechanics and dealers from throughout the USA to training courses in Milwaukee. This meant that in future, despite the increasingly complicated technology, Harley-Davidson motorcycles could be properly serviced and repaired. The production of civilian motorcycles was drastically cut and the factory's involvement in sport was temporarily halted in order to make maximum capacity available for supplying the army. Although the First World War came to an end in the year after America

stepped in, by then more than 20,000 American military motorcycles, most of them Harley-Davidsons, had been shipped to Europe, to serve as transport for American soldiers involved in reconnaissance or dispatch riding. Tradition has it that one day after the armistice of November, 11, 1918, a Harley-Davidson motorcycle and sidecar, driven by Corporal Roy Holtz, was the first American vehicle to "march" into Germany. Holtz had accidently ridden behind German lines four days previously while taking his captain to his battle position in bad weather and amid heavy fighting. When they arrived at a farmhouse where lights were burning, Holtz entered to discover where they were and fell into the hands of the troops garrisoning a German field base. The pair were taken prisoner, but were released after the armistice, returning behind their own lines just in time for the official entry of the troops into Germany.

Harley-Davidson geared production during the war very much towards the needs of the American army, but it also made sure that the civilian side was not entirely neglected. In 1917, civilian motorcycles still represented 50 per cent of the overall output at 7000 units. The big race to overtake Indian and

Excelsior, which had started before the war, was now to be successfully pursued, both at home and in Europe. The Europeans had had ample opportunity to get to know the big Harley-Davidson V-twins during the war and to compare them with the more economically designed European motorcycles. However, although the American motorcycles had won for themselves an excellent reputation in Europe, demand was slow to take off. The war had taken its toll on the various countries, incomes were low, the prices of the Harley-Davidsons were too high once import duty had been added, and the vehicle tax and insurance premiums levied in Europe on large capacity motorcycles were also too high. While the amounts of these levies were calculated in the USA according to horse power, which led to the production of large engines with relatively low specific power output and to manufacturers being restrained in their output claims, the calculations in Europe were based on cubic capacity. This put at a disadvantage the 1000cc Harley-Davidsons compared to similar European motorcycles, which frequently had only half their cubic capacity. However, after the war Harley-Davidson was confident of its leading position in

The Harley-Davidson Service School (above) was set up in 1917. The factory was concentrating at this time on the production of military machines, with new developments often being introduced to the US army by William Harley in person (left).

Roy Holtz was the first US soldier to "march" into Germany following the armistice of 11.11.1918 on a Harley-Davidson military rig.

the home market, since it had served both military and civilian markets simultaneously and equally, and had increased its efficiency in order to do so. This optimism found expression in increased publicity and the extension of production capacity. Arthur Davidson placed advertisements not only in motorcycling magazines, but also in all hobby publications which could possibly reach potential motorcycle buyers. In the late fall of 1918, work began on Harley-Davidson's 600,000 square foot, L-shaped industrial plant which provided jobs for 2,400 employees in 96 departments. The premises of the Harley-Davidson Motor Company were now larger than those of the market leader, Indian. The first step towards conquering the American motorcycle industry had been taken.

1919
An airplane belonging to the US Navy is the first to fly across the Atlantic without refueling.

1920
Women are given the vote in the USA. Warren G. Harding is elected 29th American president.

1921
Congress introduces a quota system to limit the number of immigrants.

1922
Mussolini forms the first Fascist government in Italy. *The Reader's Digest* is founded.

1923
Miguel Primo de Rivera sets up a military dictatorship in Spain. Jakob Schick patents the electric razor.

1924
Congress passes a law which makes all Indians US citizens. Adolf Hitler writes *Mein Kampf.*

1925
In Wyoming, Nellie Ross is elected first woman governor in the USA. The first edition of *The New Yorker* magazine appears.

1926
Ford introduces the 40-hour week. Gertrud Ederle is the first woman to swim the Channel.

1927
Leon Trotsky is expelled from the Communist Party of the Soviet Union.

1928
Alexander Fleming discovers penicillin. The first Mickey Mouse cartoon is made.

1929
The world economic crisis begins with "Black Friday" on the New York Stock Exchange. Emil Jannings and Janet Gaynor are awarded the first Oscars.

1930
More than 1300 American banks are forced to close. Uruguay's soccer team wins the World Cup.

1931
The number of unemployed in the USA is estimated at 14 to 15 million. In New York, the Empire State Building is finished. For 40 years it is the highest building in the world at 1250 ft.

1932
Franklin Delano Roosevelt is elected 32nd US president. Amelia Earhart is the first woman to fly alone across the Atlantic.

1933
Prohibition is lifted in the USA. Adolf Hitler becomes chancellor of Germany.

1934
Austria's chancellor Engelbert Dolfuss is murdered during an attempted *Putsch* in Vienna. Henry Miller's novel *Tropic of Cancer* is published.

1919-1934

The Flathead and the little twin

Harley-Davidson had neglected civilian production so little during the First World War that the company made a relatively smooth transition to peacetime. After a short while, only the green of the post-war motorcycles, which replaced the original gray of the Harley-Davidsons, was a reminder of the war years.

Since customers' tastes in the USA were turning increasingly towards two-cylinder machines, the single cylinder was dropped from the range and only offered from 1919 onwards in the CD model for use as a "commercial vehicle." The CD only had a 21 cubic inch (350cc) displacement and did 79 miles to the gallon. Harley-Davidson reckoned that it cost one dollar per 100 miles to run and acclaimed the CD as the ideal messenger and delivery vehicle. The factory also made suitable V-twin motorcycles for every branch of industry, some with three wheels, and offered them as an economical alternative to vans and trucks. This policy was not without success: for example, by 1924, about 1400 police stations in the USA were equipped with Harley-Davidsons, and the black and white police machines still common today are part of the American street scene.

The pre-war 61 V-twin motorcycle continued to be built largely unchanged after the war, and from 1919 onwards it was available either as an F or a J model. The F version had magneto ignition, while the J was fitted with battery ignition. In 1920, the J version was given an electrical system which had been completely developed and made at the factory, consisting of alternator, horn and electric lighting instead of the acetylene lamps that had previously been the norm. Only the battery was bought in from a supplier, but this component caused problems, so the electrical system did not function reliably, and dealers generally exchanged it without more ado for a battery made by the Remy company. At Harley-Davidson, the response was to lure a man named George Appel away from Remy and ask him to solve the problem. In the fall of 1920 the problem had been overcome and the electrical equipment on Harley-Davidsons worked reliably.

The sensation of the previous year had been the W Sport model, an agile machine weighing only 275 lbs (125kg) with a front-to-rear opposed twin Boxer engine, a 37 cubic inch (600cc) displacement and three-speed transmission. The introduction of the machine attracted just as much attention as the record-breaking ride which Julian "Hap" Scherer undertook with the Sport model on June 21, 1919. He covered the 1689 miles from the Canadian to the Mexican border in less than 65 hours. Record-breaking rides and racing successes were of great importance for sales, and were often more effective than advertising. Harley-Davidson's involvement in motor sport was accordingly considerable. Road races and enduros in the USA were dominated at that time by the special eight-valve twins developed by Bill Ottaway in the race department, and also by the standard Harley-Davidsons. In the race at Ascot Park in Los Angeles on January 4, 1920, Harley-Davidson machines took the first four places. The following month, the works team, consisting of the drivers Fred Ludlow, Leslie "Red" Parkhurst and Otto Walker took a total

The sensation of 1919: the Sport model with a 600cc flat-twin Boxer engine with enclosed final drive chain, weighing only 275 lbs (125 kg). Unfortunately, production of this promising machine was stopped in 1923.

William Davidson was the only member of the founders never to ride a motorcycle himself. He poses here in the sidecar next to William Harley (above). Even prominent contemporaries such as Prince Axel of Denmark (left) frequently had themselves photographed on a Harley-Davidson.

of 23 speed records at Daytona Beach. The astounding number of records can be explained by the fact that these were the first record attempts to be organized by the AMA (American Motorcycle Association) for which fixed rules and strict categories had been laid down. In the previous year, the FAM (Federation of American Motorcyclists) had been dissolved because of mismanagement, and at a conference of the AMMA

(American Motorcycle Manufacturers' Association), at which Harley-Davidson naturally had an important contribution to make, the AMA was founded. Nevertheless, some of the records set at Daytona Beach were very impressive: on Friday 13th no less, Red Parkhurst rode under adverse conditions – it was stormy and the sandy beach was soft – at 103 mph over one mile on a standard motorcycle. With the eight-valve racing machine he even managed nearly 111 mph over five miles. However, the great moment came on February 22, 1922 in Fresno, California, when nine out of the twelve winners were Harley-Davidson riders and when Otto Walker, for the first time in the history of the sport of motorcycling, won a race with an average speed of over 99 mph.

Harley-Davidson was even more successful in the marketplace than on the race track: about 28,000 motorcycles were sold world-wide in 1920. This achievement meant that Harley-Davidson had not only outstripped its arch rivals Excelsior and Indian, but had also become the largest motorcycle manufacturer in the world. There were authorized dealers in 67 countries, and the company magazine, *The Enthusiast*, appeared monthly in editions of 50,000 copies.

These were good times – but crisis was just around the corner, for in the meantime the blossoming economy had brought the automobile within the reach of many US citizens and most would soon be able to afford it. The motorcycle took on the image of a vehicle for people who could not afford a car, and there was a corresponding slump in sales. Of course, this first hit the smallest of the American motorcycle manufacturers, of which there were more than 200 at the time, but even Harley-Davidson's sales figures for 1921 dwindled to about 10,000 units.

The company's management was forced to streamline production and reduce the staff to 1200 employees – during the war there had been 2500 people working for Harley-Davidson. The bicycle business which, as already mentioned, was run with machines bought in from Chicago, was dropped and the spares trade for Harley-Davidson bicycles sold off to the Davis Sewing Machine Company. Harley-Davidson's involvement in motor sports was also drastically reduced for lack of money. Even so, the 1920 season cost the factory about 250,000 dollars. Officially it was said that the race department was being merged with research and development so that the racing machines would not be so far removed from the standard motorcycles and the customer could benefit more from technical advances. The company's management emphasized that they would continue to make motorcycles available to exceptionally talented riders – although to a strictly limited extent and without further benefits such as payments of prize money.

Arthur Davidson developed a basic marketing strategy to save the company, part of which involved a credit purchase scheme called "Pay as you ride."

Dealers were urged to look after their customers assiduously by organizing rides, meetings and sporting events with the aim of keeping them loyal to the marque. In 1923, Arthur Davidson even succeeded in having a secret meeting with the managers of Indian and Excelsior. At this and a subsequent meeting, price agreements were settled between the three largest American motorcycle manufacturers which were not exactly flawless in terms of cartel law. It was also agreed that every dealer would in future only be allowed to represent one marque. However, these agreements did more harm than good to the motorcycle market. Firstly, neither dealers nor customers understood or accepted that dealers should only be allowed to sell one make of motorcycle. For example, buyers always found it extremely helpful to be able to view and compare several models from different competitors in the same showroom. Secondly, exclusive trading led to the demise of the smaller motorcycle marques – which was indeed what was intended so that the three big names could divide the market between themselves.

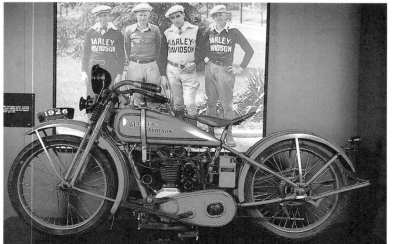

In 1922, Harley-Davidson introduced as an alternative to the 1000cc ioe V-twin a 1200cc motorcycle which was almost identical in build. In 1923, production of the Boxer and single-cylinder engines ceased, but in 1926 two new 350cc singles were launched – one of them even with an ohv engine (left).

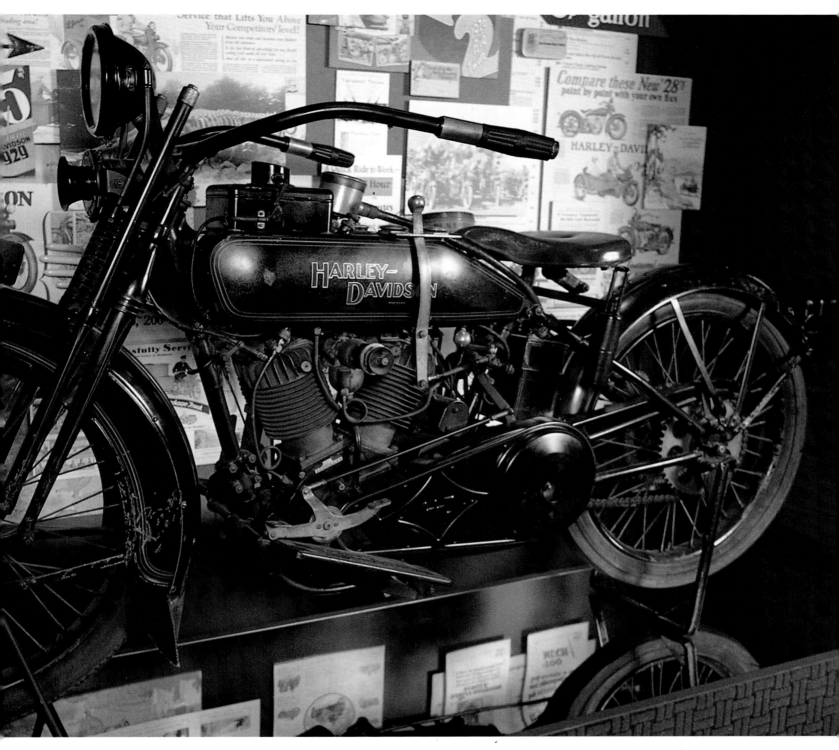

Drastic falls in turnover made it impossible for American motorcycle manufacturers to keep up with the continuing rationalization of production being carried out in the automobile industry. For purely commercial reasons, the logical step to assembly-line production was out of the question, but Harley-Davidson's founders had not lost their enthusiasm. They invested the private wealth that they had meanwhile accumulated in the company so that production could be automated – but for this they had to rethink their model policy completely. The Sport model had not got off to a good start under the declining market conditions, and sales figures remained lower than expected. In the middle of the 1922 season, production of the Boxer was therefore dropped. In 1923, only a few were still being kept ready for export since the W sold better in Britain and Australia than in the USA. Despite mediocre sales figures, the demise of the Sport model surprised many experts who thought that the motorcycle would still be successful. However, in view of the difficult economic climate, Harley-Davidson wanted to concentrate on one type of engine. Since the large volume V-twin also fitted in better with the increasingly fashionable macho image of the motorcycle, Harley-Davidson introduced in 1922 another motorcycle as an alternative to

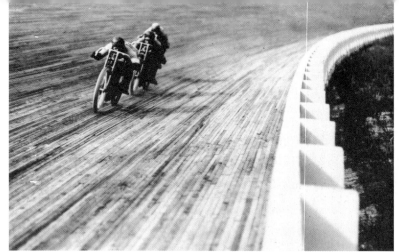

In the twenties, in addition to dirt-track and flat-track racing, board-track racing became very popular in the USA. These tracks were made from wooden planks fastened together to form high-speed ovals with raised bends.

At the end of the twenties, the racing version of the 350cc Harley-Davidson single – known as the Peashooter – was very successful on the flat tracks when ridden by riders such as Eddie Brinck, shown here.

the 61 which was technically almost identical, but with a 74 cubic inch (1200cc) displacement. This truly enormous engine for the 1920s was primarily intended for powering a sidecar and caused quite a stir on the motorcycle scene. With the two V-twin models, Harley-Davidson was well armed for the difficult twenties, during which they continually improved the specification of their motorcycles. The valve mechanism was optimized to make the engine run more smoothly, and the amount of lubricant was increased in order to improve reliability. A front wheel brake was only introduced in 1928, and at first motorcyclists greeted it with skepticism. One year later, an air filter was added with the aim of increasing the life of the engine.

However, before this, Harley-Davidson once again devoted itself to the single-cylinder engine. The reason for this was the introduction in 1925 of the Indian Prince, a 21 cubic inch (350cc) single, built along the lines of contemporary English machines. Bill Harley immediately ordered the research and development department to develop a motorcycle of the same size. One year later the machine was ready to go into production

and was offered with a choice of two engines, both of which differed from the former Harley-Davidson engines that had been exclusively ioe models until then. The basic version of the single had a side-valve engine with an iron alloy piston – inlet and exhaust valves were located beside each other next to the cylinder, and the shape of the combustion chamber followed a patent of engineer Harry Ricardo, who over the years was to make a lot of money from granting licenses. Like the big V-twins, this engine was available in an A model with magneto ignition and in a B model with battery ignition. Apart from the basic single model, there was also a sport version which had an aluminum piston and an overhead valve (ohv) mechanism – an extremely modern principle in which a cylinder's two valves hang in the cylinder head, giving an especially compact combustion chamber shape and a good inflow and outflow of gases. This version, too, could be supplied as an AA model with magneto ignition or as a BA model with battery ignition. Incidentally, the BA was the first Harley-Davidson to be fitted with

the teardrop-shaped tank which was later to be typical of the marque, a characteristic of the streamlining which was to be so important over the next few years in defining the new, modern look in motorcycle design. For the export market there were also the AAE and BAE variants with a clutch grip on the handlebars and footpegs instead of footboards.

At this time, the flat-track races that had been introduced via Australia and England from New Zealand, were becoming very popular in the USA. These were run on a flat, untarred oval, and the AA proved to be an ideal machine for such competitions. It was soon nicknamed the "Peashooter" after the small, rapid-firing revolvers of that name. Before long, Harley-Davidson was offering a true racing machine based on the AA and weighing less than 240 lbs (110kg). It had a shorter wheelbase and reinforced front forks based on the Flying Merkel, a sport motorcycle by the American Joseph Merkel that had previously been a success.

From 1928 onwards, the V-twin could also be obtained in a version with two camshafts which was simply known as the "two cam model" or JD-H. This option was available for both the 61 and the 74. These models, which were geared toward the tastes of sportier motorcyclists and were fitted with two headlamps as a special feature, did not exactly become best sellers, but were very popular because of their sportiness and reliability. Today, many vintage motorcycle enthusiasts think that the Two Cammer is one of the best models that Harley-Davidson ever built.

As with the Indian Prince and the Peashooters, so it was in 1929 that a competitor's model provided the impetus for the development of a new Harley-Davidson machine. To complete its range, Excelsior presented the 45 cubic inch (750cc) Super X, a medium-sized motorcycle developed by Arthur Constantine. Strangely enough, Constantine had previously worked as an engineer in Harley-Davidson's development department, where he had suggested just such a motorcycle. But the company, concerned as always with economy, had not only turned down his suggestion but had fired him for wasting precious time on unnecessary development. Now, however, Harley-Davidson's

Before Harley-Davidson launched the three-wheeler ServiCar onto the market in 1932, the factory was producing similar vehicles for the police service.

An enthusiasm for motorcycling was part of the job for the Davidsons – pictured here are Gordon, Walter and Allan on an 8000 mile trip in 1929.

The 1200cc V-twin was given a side-valve engine in 1930 – the Harley-Davidson Flathead was born.

response to the Super X was the 45, which also had a 750cc, side-valve, V-twin engine with a valve operating mechanism similar to that of the A and B singles. At the same time, Harley-Davidson introduced a further single-cylinder machine, which was soon given the nickname "Baby Harley," since it had the engine of the A model bored out to 500cc, but the frame of the 45. However, because of the rather over-sized frame, the Baby Harley weighed almost 440 lbs (200kg) and suffered both from mediocre performance and symptoms of overheating. Even the little twin had teething problems: the engine produced considerable torque but the the clutch and transmission had been designed in such a way that they were too weak for it. Also, the motorcycle's acceleration was not adequate to keep up with the competition. All this meant that in 1931 the 45, which was available in three versions as the basic D model, the DL touring model and the DLD Sport model, was given a more generously proportioned clutch, a strengthened transmission and a more solid frame. The previous year, the big 74 twin had also been fitted with a side-valve engine in order to keep up with the successful Indian Chief. Side-valve engines were very highly thought of at this time, especially in the automobile industry, and were known as "flatheads" because of the flat cylinder head inherent in the design. Fans of the Harley-Davidson marque also quickly adopted this nickname for the new 74. However, the new model primarily attracted attention in its early years because of numerous warranty claims. These only ceased to trouble Harley-Davidson after the engine's lubrication system had been improved and a larger clutch fitted. Until the mid-thirties, Harley-Davidson kept on trying to make the big twin more

attractive by various means, among them interchangeable wheels, a four-speed transmission, aluminum pistons, a more powerful battery, an anti-theft device on the handlebars, fork springs which could be adjusted by hand, and illuminated displays for charging current and oil pressure.

The last machine from this period of frequent new models was the three-wheeler Harley-Davidson ServiCar, which appeared in 1932. This was powered by the little twin and enjoyed immediate success as a delivery and police vehicle, even though the economic crisis had long since set in.

Since the big stock market crash of October 25, 1929, the American economy had been going steadily downhill, and the motorcycle market was heading towards an all-time low. In 1931, Excelsior went bust, and in 1933 only about 6000 motorcycles were sold in the whole of the USA, 3700 of them being Harley-Davidsons. Even the export markets dried up because most of the European countries, whose economies were also struggling, were imposing drastic protective tariffs. The

William Davidson won the Jack Pine Enduro in 1930 (facing page bottom). The 750cc V-twin ServiCar (above), introduced in 1932, met with great approval in many branches of industry.

consequences of this trend in the export market become clear if you remember that in the 1920s about half Harley-Davidson's production was for export. Besides standard motorcycles, Harley-Davidson was also exporting racing machines, with the aim of helping foreign importers win victories in motorcycle sports, and so provide publicity for the company. The first export market to close was Great Britain. The import duty on foreign vehicles was increased to 33.33 per cent, and the sole British importer of Harley-Davidson machines terminated his contract. In the course of time, most other European countries followed Britain's example. By 1934 only Holland, Belgium, a few South American countries and parts of Scandinavia and Africa remained on Harley-Davidson's export list.

During the Depression, a bitter and sometimes unfair duel was fought between Indian and Harley-Davidson. For example, after Indian, to the great disappointment of Harley-Davidson's owners, had been bought by Paul du Pont and thereby rescued from apparently certain bankruptcy, Harley-Davidson paid bonuses to all dealers who scrapped Indians. The 74 cubic inch police motorcycles were sold through special agents ex works almost at production cost. The polarization between the two remaining American motorcycle companies went so far that motorcyclists could not even buy tires, oil and other generic items in the competition's shops, and there were scuffles between members of the clubs representing the two marques, which did the image of the American motorcyclist no good whatsoever.

Harley-Davidson's management realized that the motorcycle had had its day as an inexpensive form of transport – it now cost almost as much as a Ford automobile. The only solution was to establish the motorcycle, despite the catastrophic economic situation in the USA, as a hobby, prestige and leisure item. So in 1933 Harley-Davidson began by making the dreary, almost military-looking paintwork of its motorcycles

more striking and attractive. Two- and three-color machines, with tanks painted in Art Deco style and details picked out in striking designs, heralded the meticulous paintwork which is still expected as a matter of course on Harley-Davidsons today. At the end of 1934, the factory also took the logical step of ceasing production of the single-cylinder models that had been sold primarily as an economical means of transport.

Although in the worst times of the Depression almost a third of the American working population was without a job, Harley-Davidson managed to survive without dramatically reducing its staff. Instead of this, the number of hours worked per week was reduced – often there was only enough work for two days a week, but the employees did at least have a job to go to. The extreme thriftiness of the company's management certainly contributed greatly to Harley-Davidson's survival and insured financial independence and liquidity even in times when other manufacturers had thrown in the towel. The strict dealer policy and conservative management also had a part in helping Harley-Davidson through the Depression.

1935
Congress ratifies the Social Security Law. The Nuremberg Laws are promulgated.

1936
The Spanish Civil War breaks out. Margret Mitchell publishes *Gone with the Wind*.

1937
The German airship *Hindenburg* explodes shortly before landing at Lakehurst; 36 people die. The Golden Gate Bridge is opened.

1938
Orson Well's radio play *War of the Worlds* causes panic throughout America. In the USA, a minimum hourly wage of 0.40 dollars is fixed. Child labor is prohibited.

1939
German troops invade Poland. Britain and France declare war on Germany.

1940
In the USA, foods are preserved by freeze drying for the first time. America prepares itself for imminent involvement in the Second World War by mobilizing its armed forces.

1941
The Japanese attack Pearl Harbor. Ford signs the first trade union agreement.

1942
Enrico Fermi produces the first controlled nuclear chain reaction at the University of Chicago. British and American troops attack German forces in North Africa.

1943
Allied troops land in Italy. Shoes, canned foods, meat, cheese, sugar and gasoline are rationed in the USA.

1944
US president Roosevelt is elected for the third time. Invasion of Normandy by Allied troops.

1945
Germany capitulates on 7th May. A US airplane drops the first atomic bomb on Hiroshima.

1935-1945

The Knucklehead and the Second World War

With the discontinuation of the single-cylinder models, Harley-Davidson engineers were able to concentrate entirely from 1935 onwards on overcoming the inadequacies of the 45 and 74 Flathead twins, and on developing a successor to the outdated 61 twin with its ioe valve arrangement.

The 74 really did develop into a robust, reliable engine that was primarily suited to use with a sidecar – not least because it could be supplied on request with a three-speed transmission complete with reverse gear. However, dealers held back with their orders because there was a rumor that a better model was being developed. In actual fact, Harley-Davidson did surprise the motorcycle world in 1936 with a machine derived from the 74 which had an incredible 80 cubic inch (1340cc) displacement. This enormous engine was technically identical to the 74 motor, the increase in cubic capacity simply being achieved by enlarging the bore of the cylinders. The new model was very popular because of its tremendous power. The maximum output of more than 30 hp was matched by an almost unbelievable torque at low revolutions. People's liking for the machine was not even lessened by the fact that the largest Harley-Davidson

In 1936, Harley-Davidson attracted attention with a 1340cc side-valve V-twin (above). An even more important introduction the same year was the 1000cc ohv V-twin, which was soon given the name of Knucklehead. Arthur Davidson, Walter Davidson, William S. Harley and William A. Davidson (far left) were there when the first machine rolled off the assembly line (left).

engine suffered the most from vibrations and the disadvantage inherent in the design of a V-twin, namely overheating problems in the rear cylinder, which not infrequently led to piston seizures on hot summer days. The '80s closest rival, the Indian Chief, did not suffer from these overheating problems, but was slower than the Harley-Davidson and was difficult to start on cold days.

The American economy, and with it the motorcycle market, was slowly recovering from the world economic crisis. Harley-Davidson extended its range of accessories so that motorcycle owners could give their machines individuality. Particular attention was paid to the accommodation of a pillion passenger so that motorcycling appealed as a hobby for couples. For example, extended footboards and "buddy seats" could be purchased, and it was also possible to mount a luggage carrier, panniers and a top box over the rear wheel.

The 80 cubic inch engine may have been impressive, but the technical sensation that same year was created by the introduction of the new 61. The old ioe engine had been replaced not by a Flathead but by a completely new design of engine with valves suspended in the cylinder head, in other words an ohv like the single-cylinder AA and BA models had in the 'twenties. The engine developed 36 hp from 1000cc cubic capacity, about twice as much as its predecessor, and gave the motorcycle a top speed of 90 mph – truly sensational values. It also possessed at long last a recirculating forced lubrication system which, unlike the total loss system, did not need to be constantly topped up with oil and had long been fitted as standard on Indian machines and European makes. This form of lubrication worked on a dry sump system with an oil tank containing barely one gallon of oil situated beneath the driver's seat. The shiny housing for the rockers that were connected to the ohv valve mechanism evidently made people think of the knuckles of a fist, for the machine was soon given the nickname "Knucklehead." However, it wasn't just the engine of the 61 that was new, the same applied to the four-speed transmission, the multiple-disc clutch, the strong, double-loop frame and the generously-dimensioned front forks. Of course, a price had to be paid for the sturdy construction – when filled with fuel, the motorcycle weighed 600 lbs (275kg).

The development department under Bill Harley and Bill Ottaway was proud of its success. A large part of the practical development work had been done by Joe Petralli and Hank Syvertson, who had belonged to Harley-Davidson's race department for many years. William J. Harley, the son of the company's founder, had played a part in test riding it. Like his father, he had studied engineering in Wisconsin and was now working as a designer in the factory.

However, even the new 61, of which barely 2000 were produced in 1936, did not escape teething troubles. Its main problem was that the new lubrication system suffered from leaks, but bearing damage and problems with valve gear also meant that the machine did not get off to a good start. Although American motorcycle journalists, especially those writing for the Motorcyclist, a magazine closely associated with the AMA, had praised the 61 to the skies even before the first road test was carried out, dealers and customers, who had become skeptical because of teething problems suffered by previous new models, adopted an attitude of "wait and see" towards the new motorcycle.

The problems with the first Knucklehead

model even led to Harley-Davidson halting production in Japan – a venture that, from today's point of view, would have appeared extremely promising. The background to the Japanese plant was as follows: when Harley-Davidson exposed irregularities in the conduct of the sole Japanese importer, Nippon Jidoshe of Tokyo, it founded the Harley-Davidson Sales Company of Japan, which achieved remarkable successes under the management of Alfred "Rich" Child. However, when in 1929 the yen's value against the dollar dropped by more than 50 per cent and the company was about to be abandoned because of the Japanese market's loss of attractiveness, Child convinced Harley-Davidson's management to allow motorcycles to be made in Japan instead. Harley-Davidson granted the necessary licenses to the Sankyo company which, with the aid of workshop drawings and parts lists from the USA, produced motorcycles in a factory in Shinagawa. When Harley-Davidson insisted that Sankyo also acquire the licenses for the new ohv twin, the Japanese refused after long discussions to take on this as yet not fully mature model, and this led eventually to a complete rift between the companies. Harley-Davidson terminated the cooperation and appointed Child sole importer for Japan, Korea, North China and Manchuria, while Sankyo continued to produce the 61 with ioe engine in its Shinagawa factory. The machine did not bear the name of Harley-Davidson, but was known as *Rikuo*, which means "King of the Road."

Meanwhile, in Milwaukee, the engineers were hard at work eliminating the weaknesses of the new 61 – for one thing, almost all the valve gear components

In an effort to boost the popularity of the Knucklehead, which had suffered teething problems, Joe Petralli, a member of the works racing team, took many records in 1937 on a specially prepared machine (left). However, the Flatheads continued to be favored by the customers – as was the "little" 750cc twin (above).

were replaced. Dealers were supplied with these parts so that they could replace them on machines brought into the workshop with damage to this particular mechanism.

Finally, a record-breaking ride was once more undertaken to prove the performance of the new motorcycle. Sylvertson and Petralli prepared a Knucklehead to win back the mile record on Daytona Beach, Florida, which had been pushed up to more than 125 mph in 1932 by Johnny Seymour on an Indian. The motorcycle was fitted with a bar-mounted fairing, a disc wheel in front and a cover extending from the engine block to the rear of the machine. This meant that the aerodynamics were improved, but the new engine was protected neither from the head wind nor from the eyes of the public. On the first attempt, Petralli was only just able to avert a fall, because the machine's coverings had impaired its stability. For the second attempt, he had the aerodynamic aids removed and set a sensational record of 136.18 mph, which to this day has never been repeated on sand. Apart from record breaking, the use of motorcycles for sport was growing again with the improving economic situation. Racing had obviously lost none of its advertising potential. Harley-Davidson's activities could not be compared with those before the Depression, but even with its restricted involvement there were many successes in the AMA's A and B categories for professional racing motorcyclists as well as category C for racing amateurs. Harley-Davidson riders carried off the prizes for classic road races, long-distance races, dirt-track races, hillclimbs, enduros and even trials meetings, a type of racing imported from Great Britain.

The most popular Harley-Davidson machine with the amateurs was the 45, which had meanwhile been perfected to such an extent that it could more than

In 1941, a 1200cc ohv motorcycle was introduced – the forerunner of the FL models.

stand comparison with the Indian Scout. But even the old 61 with its ioe engine was greatly loved as a sports motorcycle, and its owners, who distrusted the reliability of the new ohv models, stocked up with piles of spares for their favorite discontinued model so they could carry on racing it for as long as possible. This of course went against the interests of the factory, since the intention was to disperse the ohv 61 as quickly as possible among active sports riders. Harley-Davidson therefore used its influence with the AMA to change the rules so that ioe engines were banned in future from the C class. Many sports riders were annoyed at this step, but Harley-Davidson's generous financial support of the AMA was paying off, and it continued to increase its influence over the association until it reached a peak in 1944 with the election of Arthur Davidson as AMA president.

With the popularity of motor sports in the second half of the 1930s, motorcycle clubs in the USA experienced a tremendous upturn. Sports club members mostly rode stripped down sport machines, light motorcycles such as the Indian Scout or Harley-Davidson 45, from which all superfluous components had been removed in order to increase performance as much as possible. Alongside this, a new scene grew up with the advent of the touring clubs. Their members preferred the so-called "full dresser," generally large-capacity Harley-

Davidsons fitted with windshield, dual seat, panniers, additional headlamps and every conceivable accessory designed to make touring more pleasant. There was even a motorcycle club for women, the Motor Maids of America, with local branches in all the large cities in the USA, founded and run by Verena Griffith, a Harley-Davidson rider. Her deputy was Dorothy Robinson, wife of the Detroit Harley-Davidson dealer Earl Robinson.

The strong orientation of the club scene towards Milwaukee was further confirmed by most of the clubs being connected with the AMA, which in turn was heavily influenced by Harley-Davidson.

In the late 1930s, the two reworked big Flathead models were far more readily accepted than the Knucklehead, especially by the touring enthusiasts. The Flatheads were now also fitted with recirculating lubrication systems. At a little more than 30 hp and weighing 660 lbs (300kg), they

were not among the fastest and most maneuverable motorcycles of their time, but their ease of maintenance, reliability and durability is still praised by vintage motorcycle enthusiasts today.

On April 21, 1936, the Harley-Davidson community was shocked to hear of William Davidson's death following a relatively short illness. The company's vice president had been a heavily built, corpulent man who liked eating well and was partial to a brand of beer brewed in Milwaukee. After his first stay in hospital, the oldest of the Davidson brothers should have radically altered his way of life, but he disregarded his doctors' advice. William Davidson had finally become completely immobilized by a circulatory disorder which caused his legs to swell up. When doctors attempted to save his life by amputating both legs, he failed to recover from the anaesthetic.

For the first time, and after more than three decades, someone took over a managerial role at Harley-Davidson who was not one of the company's founders. Bill Ottaway was appointed as the new works manager. He took over from William Davidson in difficult times, for the trade unions were becoming increasingly powerful in the USA at the end of the 1930s and even put Harley-Davidson under considerable pressure. Ottaway negotiated a contract with the United Auto Workers Union which increased wages by 15 per cent and forced the company's management to put motorcycle prices up by 10 per cent. It is true that the workers were now earning more, but if one can believe contemporary reports, the atmosphere in the conservatively managed company,

About 80,000 WLA 45 Harley-Davidsons, a military version of the 750cc V-twin, arrived in Europe during the Second World War.

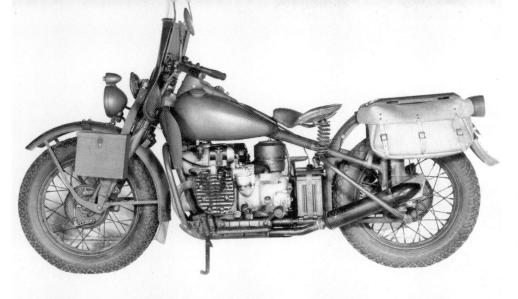

Only a few XA 45 models, which were built along the lines of the BMW military motorcycles, were ever put into service.

which until then had been that of a large family, suffered because of the power of the unions and the death of the vice president.

Over the next few years, old and modern production methods were used side by side at Harley-Davidson. Almost all the parts used to make the motorcycles were manufactured at the factory – many of them using traditional skills. Also, since the bad years of the Depression, motorcycles were only assembled once an order had been placed, so that there was no need for expensive storage space for finished machines, and the customer's wishes regarding paintwork and equipment could be taken into account.

In order to comply with such wishes still more effectively, Harley-Davidson offered on all models from 1940 onwards the option of 16 inch wheels with five-inch wide tires. These gave a more comfortable ride because of the larger tire volume. Also, the 61 was fitted as standard, and the 45 and 74 optionally, with aluminum cylinder heads which were lighter and conducted the heat of the engine away more effectively than cast iron heads. In the fall of 1940, the sensation for the following season was unveiled: a 74 cubic inch version of the Knucklehead with more than 45 hp, which was to be offered in the chassis of the well-known 74 alongside the Flathead. However, before sufficient examples of this motorcycle could be sold to prove that it was the first standard Harley-Davidson to be capable of travelling at 100 mph, the factory had to turn its production almost completely

over to manufacturing arms because, following the Japanese attack on Pearl Harbor, the USA had entered the Second World War.

Ever since 1939, when war broke out in Europe, Harley-Davidson and Indian had been receiving substantial orders from Europe for military motorcycles, as European motorcycle production had already been largely brought to a standstill by bombardments. Harley-Davidson turned the 45 into a machine suitable for war. It was fitted with 18 inch wheels that were more suitable for rough terrain, wide mudguards and a large air filter. The engine was also protected from below by a large steel sump guard, and the transmission was given an extra low-ratio gear to facilitate slow, cross-country riding. With luggage carrier, panniers and provision for carrying a rifle and ammunition, this motorcycle, known as the WLA 45, was so heavy that it could barely go faster than 50 mph, but its ease of maintenance and high degree of reliability contributed to its great success in military use. When the US army's orders started coming in, additional factory space had to be rented and new workers taken on.

The US army, which had been impressed by the performance of the BMW Boxer motorcycles during German General Erwin Rommel's African campaign, asked the American motorcycle industry to build a comparable vehicle. Harley-Davidson presented the XA 45 in 1942, a motorcycle with a flat-twin, side-valve, 750cc Boxer engine, foot-operated four-speed transmission, hand-operated clutch and Cardan shaft – a carbon copy of the BMW. However, the army's initial interest

in this, the only Harley-Davidson to have a Cardan shaft, soon faded when problems appeared with the lubrication system and valve gear. Only 1000 units were ever built, while Harley-Davidson produced a total of 88,000 motorcycles – the majority of them WLAs – during the course of the Second World War. At the end of the war, it still had parts for 33,000 more machines in its warehouse. For this remarkable contribution to the nation's military equipment, the "E-Award" of the US Army and Navy for "excellent services" was twice bestowed on Harley-Davidson.

However, the company's president was not able to receive this award: Walter Davidson became seriously ill during the war. Liver disease, and overwork resulting from the expansion brought about by the armaments orders, took a lot out of the president, who had always been a difficult person to work with, but vital to the company. He never recovered and died on February 7, 1942 at the age of 65. There was some speculation as to who would succeed him, and there was a considerable delay before the appointment as second president of William Herbert Davidson, son of the vice president William A. Davidson who had died in 1937. A graduate in business management, the new president of the Harley Davidson Motor Company was an enthusiastic motorcyclist.

In the fall of the following year, on September 18, 1943, the Harley-Davidson community received another shock: William Harley also died, at the age of only 63. He suffered a heart attack in the bar of a Milwaukee club. Harley was the father of the first Harley-Davidson motorcycles and possessed a very versatile intellect. He was passionately devoted to his job as an engineer, and combined technical knowledge with an ability to think abstractly and come up with new designs. He spent what little spare time he had on painting and drawing. His position as chief engineer was initially taken over by Bill Ottaway, then by his son William J. Harley, who had already worked for two years as his father's assistant.

So, of the four founders of the Harley-Davidson Motor Company, only Arthur Davidson survived the Second World War, and he was not to be granted a long life either.

1946
The first UN general assembly meets in London.

1947
US Captain Chuck Yeager breaks the sound barrier with the rocket-powered airplane *Bell X 1*. The transistor is invented at the Bell Telephone Laboratories.

1948
Berlin is blockaded by the USSR; British and American planes supply the city via an air bridge. Mahatma Gandhi is assassinated.

1949
The North Atlantic Treaty is signed by 12 nations. Mao Tse-tung proclaims the Peoples' Republic of China.

1950
Start of the Korean War.

1951
US president Harry S. Truman recalls General Douglas McArthur as Commander in Chief of UN forces in Korea.

1952
Dwight D. Eisenhower is elected 34th president of the USA. The USA explodes the first hydrogen bomb in Eniwetok Atoll.

1953
The Korean War comes to an end. Arthur Miller's play *The Crucible* accuses McCarthy of leading a witch hunt against Communists in the USA.

1954
In the USA, the first nuclear-powered submarine *Nautilus* is launched. The first vaccinations against polio are given in the USA.

1955
The USA starts supporting the South Vietnamese Army in the war against North Vietnam.

1956
The first Transatlantic telephone cable is put into operation.

1957
The USSR launches the first space satellite, *Sputnik I*. Six nations found the EEC in Rome.

1958
The Americans launch their first satellite, *Explorer I*. Jack S. Kilby builds the first electronic chip in the USA.

1959
Alaska and Hawaii become the 49th and 50th Federal States of the USA. The Communist Fidel Castro seizes power in Cuba.

1960
The USA launches a total of 17 satellites into space. Francis G. Powers is shot down in an American U2 spy plane over Russia.

1961
The USA breaks off diplomatic relations with Cuba and supports the counter-revolutionary invasion in the Bay of Pigs, which, however, fails.

1962
John Glenn is the first American astronaut in space. The USA sets up a sea blockade against Cuba because of Soviet missiles stationed there.

1963
US president John F. Kennedy is assassinated in Dallas, Texas.

1964
Opposition to the Vietnam War begins in American universities.

1946-1964

The Panhead and the Sportster

After the Second World War had come to an end in 1945, there was a great demand for motorcycles in the USA. Above all, men returning from the war were looking for adventure of a peaceful kind. At first, large numbers of ex-military machines, some of them brand new, were sold off to ordinary people, thus temporarily satisfying the demand. The army sold a total of 15,000 WLA models with the 750cc big V-twin engine for 450 dollars each and the XA Boxer machines fetched 500 dollars. Many dealers bought these motorcycles in large numbers and offered them for resale in their shops – either in their original configuration or converted to civilian machines. At Harley-Davidson there were still large stocks of spares and unassembled military machines, and it was 1947 before the factory could concentrate entirely on the production of civilian motorcycles again.

The overall economic situation in the USA at this time was greatly affected by the total economic collapse in Europe, for an important market had been lost to the export-dependent American economy. In addition, the specter of Communism was hovering over Europe, and the American government under President Harry S. Truman decided to give the economy of Western

The second and third generations of the founding family in 1949: William H. Davidson on a new Hydra Glide with 1200cc Panhead engine flanked by his sons John A. (left) and William G. (right) on 125cc two-stroke Harley-Davidsons.

Europe a boost with the aid of the Marshall Plan. Under this European Recovery Programme, considerable proportions of America's output of raw materials, for example, steel, iron, aluminum and other light metals, were shipped to Europe. At the same time, import duty on finished products was lowered. This did not make the situation for American industry any easier. In order to give American companies a degree of security, the government guaranteed them a supply of raw materials equal to that which they had received in the last years before the war. For Harley-Davidson this was not a good basis from which to defend itself against the pressure of competition from increasing imports from Europe. In 1946, almost 10,000 foreign motorcycles were sold in the USA, most of them of British origin. Among the importers was a not insignificant proportion of men who had previously worked for Harley-Davidson and who knew exactly where the weaknesses of their old firm lay. However, there was also an advantage in these imports, for they increased the range of machines on offer and thus helped to liven up the American motorcycle market considerably.

Under these circumstances – with limited supplies of raw materials, collapsed export markets and strong competition on the home market – Harley-Davidson began only limited production of three pre-war models: the two 61 and 74 cubic inch ohv models and the 45 with its side-valve engine. Apart from these, the 74 Flathead could be manufactured on request, but no longer appeared in the official range, and the same applied to the ServiCar, various combinations with sidecars and delivery vehicles. Since demand on the motorcycle market exceeded the number of available motorcycles, the factory supplied dealers on a quota basis.

Harley-Davidson tried to meet the stiff competition with high standards of quality and a strict dealer policy. For example, the steel parts of the motorcycles were subjected to the Parker Process, a form of anticorrosion protection previously developed by Edward Parker in premises rented from Indian. The dealers were required to swear loyalty to the marque and promote the Harley-Davidson image. They were even forbidden to maintain or repair other makes of motorcycle in their workshops. The factory disseminated the doctrine of pure, traditional motorcycling in the American spirit. It appealed to motorcyclists to uphold American tradition and support American industry. An event of far-reaching importance in 1947 for American motorcycling and for the motorcyclist's image was the General Clubmen's Meeting which was held for the first time on 4th July in Hollister, California and now takes place annually. Over 4000 motorcyclists gathered there, among them a relatively small group of outlaws who terrorized the meeting, the town and the whole area throughout the weekend. The police had to bring in 500 officers to provide at least some protection for the townspeople. The press, of course, had a field day. *Life* magazine published a detailed report on the outlaw clubs and showed on the cover of its edition the photo of an obviously drunk Harley Davidson rider, sitting on his motorbike with a bottle of beer in his hand. The 25th anniversary edition of the magazine showed this photo on its cover for a second time.

The events at Hollister aroused in people a partly unjustified prejudice against motorcyclists, but they also illustrated that motorcycle clubs had to some extent become a reservoir for antisocial elements. The outlaws mostly rode Harley-Davidson big twins, though in a stripped version. The habit of replacing motorcycle parts by lighter ones or removing them altogether began in California. There, such machines were known as "bobbers." Members of straight clubs, on the other hand, mostly possessed "dressers," motorcycles with a multitude of accessories such as windshield, panniers, additional headlamps and crash bars. Since many Harley-Davidson dealers refused to serve outlaws, workshops sprang up which specialized in this type of clientele, where it was not unusual for stolen motorcycles and spares to be traded. This scene developed into a real problem for Harley-Davidson.

Despite all the adversities during these years, the people at Harley-Davidson had not given up and development of the big twin continued. Efforts were primarily geared towards eliminating the overheating problems and oil leaks once and for all. In 1947, a new engine was introduced which had aluminum cylinder heads and used push-rod type hydraulic lifters in the valve train. From 1948, both the big twin models, the 61 and the 74, were fitted with the new engine which was given the nickname "Panhead," because its cylinder head covers looked like overturned cake-pans. However, even the Panhead had its teething troubles: in the initial phase it sometimes happened that the oil pump did not build up enough pressure to insure that the hydraulic push rods functioned, resulting in rattling valve gear and a drop in performance due to altered timings.

In November 1947 Harley-Davidson organized a general meeting of all its American dealers – the largest meeting of its kind in the factory's history – to make them renew their oath of allegiance and to make two new strategies attractive to them. One strategy became clear when William J. Harley presented to the dealers the prototype of a lightweight 125cc two-stroke machine with three-speed transmission and rubber-band suspension which was a fairly close imitation of the German pre-war DKW. The patents for the engine, which BSA in Britain was shortly also to build, were secured by the two companies when they acquired German investments following the country's capitulation. Harley-Davidson hoped to increase its options with this cheap motorcycle and proudly showed the dealers a factory building in the Milwaukee suburb of Wauwatosa that had been bought from the government to house its production. To put it briefly, the two-stroke motorcycle only enjoyed a limited success. In 1953, the cubic capacity was increased to 165cc and the motorcycle was enhanced by hydraulic telescopic forks, but in 1962 production was finally stopped.

Harley-Davidson's other new strategy was to increase involvement in sport. The dealers at the Milwaukee meeting were called upon to increase their sponsorship. The factory announced increased production of the WR racing machine and asked dealers to do everything to prevent foreign marques from dominating. As far as the AMA's regulations were concerned, Harley-Davidson was still able to exert a powerful influence, and promising sport bikes such as the Ariel Red Hunter and the Triumph Speed Twin were prevented from competing with the side-valve Harley-Davidsons by clever additions to the rules. Road races on asphalt were dismissed as too dangerous – such races had long been held in Europe, so European manufacturers

After the 1200cc Panhead had been given hydraulically damped telescopic forks and the attractive name of Hydra Glide in 1949, the 750cc Harley-Davidson was given a more comfortable chassis in 1952 which even boasted rear wheel suspension. However, this modern concept does not blend all that well with the out-dated, low-powered Flathead engine of the K model shown here.

In 1954, the K progressed to the KH, and the side-valve engine was bored out to 900cc. However, it wasn't until three years later, in 1957, that the small ohv engine was ready for production – the KH evolved into the first Sportster, shown here, which was immediately given an enthusiastic reception.

The success of the Sportster came at just the right time for the factory, when there were just two four-stroke models in the Harley-Davidson range – apart from the 900cc Sportster, there was only the 1200cc Hydra Glide. In 1958, the big twin was also given rear wheel suspension and from then on was known as the Duo Glide, shown here.

Harley-Davidson's magazine for its customers, The Enthusiast, was established in 1916, and is the oldest motorcycle magazine in the USA today. Elvis Presley poses on a KH for the cover of the 5/56 edition.

could be expected to have an advantage when it came to expertise.

For the next two years the formula worked. Harley-Davidson riders won 19 out of 23 possible victories in 1948 in the national championship races, and in 1949 – the year in which Harley-Davidson equipped the 74 with hydraulically damped telescopic forks instead of the usual Springer forks and hit upon the elegant name of "Hydra Glide" – it took 17 out of the 24 first places in the championships. Only the victory of a British Norton ridden by Billy Mathews in Daytona ended the run of Harley-Davidson victories in 1950 and plunged the race department into feverish activity. A new, more competitive racing machine had to be developed.

The year 1950 did not get off to a good start for Harley-Davidson in Daytona, and it ended very badly in Milwaukee. On 30th December a motorcyclist traveling at high speed strayed onto the wrong side of the road and crashed head-on into an oncoming car. The car's two occupants were hurled from their vehicle and died of their injuries: they were Arthur Davidson and his wife. The company had now lost the last of the four founding members, a man who had helped Harley-Davidson through difficult times with his passionate, almost pathological antipathy towards all competitors. Arthur Davidson's successor as general sales manager was his nephew, Walter Davidson Jr. The post of AMA president was taken over by George D. Gilbert, who at the same time moved jobs

from the Baldwin-Duckworth Chain Company in Springfield, Massachusetts, to Harley-Davidson.

The race department adopted many details from the European competition for its new racing machine, which was called the KR. It had foot-operated gears, a hand-operated clutch and rear wheel suspension, but its engine was still the outdated side-valve little twin, and victories proved difficult to win with the new machine. It took until 1954 and required the assistance of the famous tuner Tom Sifton before a Harley-Davidson rider in the person of Joe Leonard again won the national championship, which was held that year for the first time according to a new AMA points scheme.

Even before this, in 1952, improvements to the racing machine had been incorporated in the 45 cubic inch roadster which was known as the model K. Its main features were four-speed transmission which was located in a joint housing with the engine's crank mechanism, hydraulically damped telescopic forks as on the Hydra Glide and rear wheel suspension. The comfortably sprung chassis was a concession to the spirit of the age, but powered as it was by an obsolete engine, which in principle dated back to the 1920s, the model K did not prove a success. In order to give the motorcycle at least an acceptable level of performance, the cubic capacity was increased two years later from 750 to 900cc, this model being known as the KH.

Harley-Davidson had finally stopped production of the 74 Flathead and the 61 Panhead in 1952, and the 74 Panhead underwent some changes. For example, the hydraulic lifters which had originally been located in the cylinder head were placed beneath the push rods, and a camshaft with different timings was used. The big twin was also available on request with foot-operated gear change and hand clutch instead of the tank gearshift and foot clutch which had previously been the norm. With this new Panhead, the ohv twin at last became a reliable, robust and powerful engine which the company proudly compared on the occasion of its 50th anniversary in 1953 to the contemporary V8 engines of the automobile manufacturers Ford, Chrysler and General Motors.

That same year, Indian, the only American motorcycle manufacturer to

have kept going alongside Harley-Davidson, closed its doors for lack of prospects on the motorcycle market. And indeed, Harley-Davidson found things increasingly difficult. Competition from Europe was strong, and what was to confront the Americans from the Far East could not even have been guessed at when the November edition of the motorcycle magazine *Cycle* carried the first advertisement, which promised: "You meet the nicest people on a Honda."

In contrast, Harley-Davidson riders were not considered to be the nicest people by the average American, and their image was still suffering as a result of the outlaw scene. The outlaws' bikes had meanwhile come to be known as "choppers" because they often looked as though parts had simply been chopped off in the stripping process. It was not exactly beneficial to the Harley-Davidson image that many Harley-Davidson riders liked and copied these choppers and macho image of the outlaw, without in fact belonging to this shady group. These people, who generally were not organized into clubs, were known in the 1950s as "bikers," a name by which almost every motorcyclist in the USA likes to be known today. Gradually the term "custom bike" began to be applied to the bikers' individually done-up machines, for they were custom made by a dealer or by the customer himself.

The 1950s were truly difficult for Harley-Davidson. The company had problems with its image, and there were now only two models in its range, the KH and Hydra Glide, with the smaller machine holding little attraction due to its totally outdated engine. From time to time annual production sank below 10,000 units, and the research and development department was working feverishly on a successor to the KH. This was presented in 1957, and finally in the modern chassis there was an engine to match – a 900cc ohv. The Sportster was born and was immediately received with enthusiasm by the customers. This was hardly surprising, since the engine had been designed along the lines of the Chevrolet motto, "one hp per cubic inch." The Sportster developed 55 hp and weighed barely 440 lbs (200kg) – that was a sensational performance to weight ratio and won much admiration for

Harley-Davidson from sports-minded customers. From the following year onwards, the Sportster was known by the letters XLH, and an even sportier version was released as an alternative to it, the XLCH. Also in 1958, the Hydra Glide, which until then still had a fixed rear wheel, was given hydraulically damped rear suspension and became known as the Duo Glide.

With the two 900cc Sportsters and the 1200cc Duo Glide, Harley-Davidson now had three competitive motorcycles on the market, but no further models were forthcoming which could contribute to a significant increase in market share. For this reason, the company management seized the opportunity in the summer of 1960 and bought 50 per cent of the shares in the Italian motorcycle company Aermacchi when it got into financial difficulties. Harley-Davidson itself was not exactly lying on a bed of roses, but the strength of the dollar eased the burden of the purchase, and production costs were low in Italy. The company Aermacchi-Harley-Davidson S.A. was then set up in Switzerland. Over the next 18 years a whole range of models between 50 and 350cc was produced under this name and the machines were introduced onto the American market as Shortster, Baja and Leggero. These were mostly scramblers – road machines with high exhaust, high handlebars and high profile tires which gave them some ability to cope with rough terrain. However, the range also included a motor scooter with plastic bodywork and centrifugal clutch. The first product of this American-Italian alliance to be

This, too, is a Harley-Davidson: the Super 10 from 1960, with a 165cc two-stroke engine.

exported to America in 1961 was the Aermacchi Ala Verde. It had a 250cc four-stroke engine and was renamed Sprint for the American market. During the 1960s, Harley-Davidson developed a further sphere of activity. Golf, and gasoline-driven or electric golf carts, were

Harley-Davidson's futile attempt to gain a foothold in the small machine market involved the purchase of the Italian marque Aermacchi in 1960. The Topper scooter was introduced that same year – the photograph shows a 1963 model.

becoming increasingly popular, and the Milwaukee factory started producing such vehicles. Since increasing proportions of plastic parts were being used for these three- or four-wheeled vehicles and also for motorcycles, Harley-Davidson bought up the Tomahawk Boat Company, a manufacturer of boat hulls in Tomahawk, Wisconsin, and set up the production of plastic parts there.

Meanwhile, the American racing scene was again being dominated by Harley-Davidson. The legendary Carrol Resweber from Cedarburg, Wisconsin, won almost every race he entered, securing the championship title for Harley-Davidson from 1958 to 1961, until he suffered a bad accident in 1962. However, publicity from sporting successes was not nearly as effective as in the pre-war period, and by the middle of the 1960s the Milwaukee company had its fair share of worries.

1965
More than 2600 people are arrested following an anti-racist demonstration in Selma, Alabama. The USA starts bombing North Vietnam.

1966
LSD becomes a modern drug. Michael E. De Bakey implants an artificial heart into a person for the first time.

1967
China explodes its first hydrogen bomb. The number of American soldiers in Vietnam totals 475,000.

1968
Martin Luther King Jr. and Senator Robert F. Kennedy are assassinated. Bob Beaman jumps 8.90 meters in Mexico and sets a fabulous world record for the long jump.

1969
The American feature film *Easy Rider* becomes a worldwide success. Neil A. Armstrong is the first man to step onto the moon.

1970
Senate revokes the "Tonkin Resolution" which empowered the US president to wage war in Southeast Asia. Salvador Allende wins the presidential elections in Chile.

1971
The voting age in the USA is lowered to 18 years. The rock opera *Jesus Christ Superstar* is given its first performance in New York.

1972
US president Nixon and the Soviet head of state Brezhnev sign the SALT I agreement in Moscow. Nixon meets Mao Tse-tung in Peking.

1973
US vice president Agnew resigns because of tax evasion, his successor is Gerald Ford. The last US troops leave Vietnam on 29th March.

1965-1973

The Shovelhead and the first custom bikes

By the mid 1960s it was clear that Harley-Davidson was coming under increasing pressure from competition in the Far East. Apart from Honda, names such as Yamaha, Suzuki, Kawasaki and Bridgestone were appearing on the American market. All were offering a range of small, powerful and attractive two-stroke machines. The Japanese were quick to recognize that the US market was not particularly receptive to mopeds and small motorcycles. Soon Honda led the way with a 250cc model named Hawk and a 350cc model known as Dream. Both machines were given a reasonable reception by American motorcycle riders.

These machines generally suffered from technical defects and were not among the most reliable, but they offered an excellent level of horsepower at a favorable price and were bought primarily by large numbers of young Americans.

Harley-Davidson was barely able to defend itself against the growing pressure of competition, even though it had three models in its range with the two Sportster versions and the Duo Glide. The Duo Glide was given an electric starter in 1965 following the Japanese example, and from then on it was known as the Electra Glide. As part of the improvements to the 1200cc motorcycle, the electrical system was converted from 6 volts to 12 volts, and the power output of the Panhead was boosted from 52 to 65 hp by changing the timing and increasing the compression. However, this added considerably to the engine's vibrations.

The proportion of Harley-Davidsons on the American motorcycle market was only six per cent in 1965, and turnover for the same year was a meager 30 million dollars – a devastating result which could hardly

This was not surprising, since these motorcycles were astonishingly cheap thanks to low production costs in Japan, and they also offered an electric starter – an unheard-of luxury by the standards of the time. Moreover, Japanese products soon earned the reputation of being very reliable – for example, engine leaks, such as were always recurring with American and British machines, were unheard of in Japanese motorcycles.

Even the British competition was not idle: Matchless, Norton, BSA and Triumph introduced 650 and 750cc four-stroke machines which were direct competitors for the Harley-Davidson Sportster models.

Another attempt at a two-stroke machine: the 1966 Bobcat (left) with a 175cc engine. The Aermacchi four-stroke motorcycles were responsible for a number of records and sporting successes in the sixties – ridden by "Black Bart" Markel (facing page), US champion in 1962, '65 and '66, and by George Roedern (below), world record rider in '65.

There were also Harley-Davidson two-stroke machines in the 'seventies, made by Aermacchi, such as this Baja 100 from 1971.

be expected to bring in large profits. The company needed capital more than anything else just to get back firmly on its feet. Harley-Davidson's management therefore decided to go public and offer company shares for sale. The Harley and Davidson families understandably made sure that they retained a majority of the shares so that strangers would not take control of the firm. However, despite all efforts, the financial results remained modest.

While the managers were wringing their hands and looking for solutions, the engineers were not idle. They revised the big twin with a view to a further increase in output. They designed new cylinder heads with new ports and more compact combustion chambers which contributed to higher compression, as well as new camshafts which led to longer valve opening times. A year after its renaming, the Electra Glide was given this new engine, which Harley-Davidson fans christened the "Shovelhead," because the shape of the cylinder head covers reminded them of the overturned blade of a coal shovel.

While the factory continued to distance itself from the customization movement in the USA, interest was nevertheless growing in the customized bobbers and choppers, most of which were still Harley-Davidsons. Shows were held, and there was even a magazine called *Street*

Chopper to cater for owners of such bikes. The once small, back-street dealers, who supplied custom riders with aftermarket parts because most official dealers refused to serve them, developed into real entrepreneurs who copied the expensive Harley-Davidson spares in large quantities and offered them to customers at cheap prices. Although the company did not want to admit it, by the end of the 'sixties bikers with their custom machines were responsible for a considerable part of the Harley-Davidson image. The movement was reflected in a series of Hollywood films with famous stars, in which bikers, most of them genuine ones, played subordinate roles or appeared as extras. When *Easy Rider*, starring Peter Fonda, Dennis Hopper and Jack Nicholson became a cult film, the idea of the biker movement spread right around the world. Harley-Davidson thus became an indispensable part of the biker image, but the company itself did not participate in all this. Instead, it was suffering because of the increasing number of companies who were making aftermarket parts for custom bikes and copying original spares, thereby making life difficult for Harley-Davidson as well as for authorized dealers who had remained loyal to the marque. Harley-Davidson's difficulties took a dramatic turn for the worse, especially since the export business, which had previously been so important, had

never recovered after the Second World War. For example, in the 1968 financial year it made up a meager three per cent. Finally, the management of the last remaining American motorcycle manufacturer, which provided a means of earning a living for 1700 employees and 650 dealers in the USA and Canada, saw joining forces with a larger, healthier concern as the only means of saving the company. Two companies showed an interest in such a merger: the American Machine and Foundry Company, known as AMF, and the Bangor-Punta group. Apart from industrial machines for various applications, both companies produced leisure equipment such as boats, yachts and camping requisites.

Bangor-Punta was buying up all the Harley-Davidson shares it could get hold of in order to achieve a majority shareholding as quickly as possible, thus causing the share price to soar. However, President William H. Davidson advised shareholders to accept AMF's offer. The plan was for a tax-free exchange of Harley-Davidson shares against AMF shares while retaining the current management, who would also be permitted to work independently in future. After some argument, which further pushed up the price of Harley-Davidson shares, to the benefit of the shareholders, the body of shareholders decided to follow the

In 1971, Harley-Davidson made an important move when it brought out the FX 1200 Super Glide, a cross between the Sportster and the Electra Glide.

president's advice. AMF officially took over Harley-Davidson on January 7, 1969. As agreed, hardly anything changed in the company structure in order to make a show of continuity. William H. Davidson remained as president, William J. Harley as vice president and head of engineering, and Walter Davidson Jr. as second vice president and head of sales. The third generation of the founders' families was already represented on the management by the president's two sons, John A. and William G. Davidson.

Harley-Davidson had been saved, but AMF soon began a critical analysis of the family firm and uncovered numerous irregularities. For example, there was the blinkered management which consisted almost exclusively of members of the founders' families who had risen to key positions, sometimes despite the lack of qualifications. Then there were the hopelessly outdated pre-war production plants – modernization would have meant taking out a loan from a commercial bank, something which the company's management had repeatedly refused to do from the outset. There was also the marketing plan that was based on the traditional ideal of the motorcyclist, thereby unduly limiting the target group. Every biker on a custom bike was equated with outlaws and not accepted

as a Harley-Davidson customer, even though custom bikers were the greatest worshippers of the Harley-Davidson cult. Finally, there was the company's "take it or leave it" policy with dealers, which was not exactly guaranteed to attract the long-term loyalty of the best of them. AMF therefore found a company which was in need of basic reorganization, but which had been promised that all the managers would remain at their posts. First of all, AMF's management saw to it that an extensive advertising campaign for Harley-Davidson motorcycles was carried out and that modern tools were purchased and production boosted. The plan was to expand production in the long term with new marketing strategies. However, considerably more remained as it had been than was good for the firm. For example, the lightweight Aermacchi-Harley-Davidson motorcycles were kept in the range, although they had not been a success on the US market because American motorcyclists preferred machines with a larger cubic capacity. Even dealers did not consider the small single-cylinder machines to be proper motorcycles, and their sales talk accordingly failed to convince the customers.

Harley-Davidson's traditional involvement in motorcycle racing, which was as successful as ever at the end of the sixties but was no longer effective as a means of

advertising, also continued unchanged after the merger. In 1968, Cal Rayborn won the prestigious Daytona race with a record average speed of 100 mph. Harley-Davidson riders won a total of 18 out of 23 US championship races during that season. Although the first Japanese bikes were making an appearance at the dirt-track races, the outdated, side-valve model K racing machines were still in a position to win. At Harley-Davidson, they knew that this would not be the case for much longer, so they got the head of the race department, Dick O'Brien, to develop a racing machine from the ohv Sportster – the 62 hp XR 750. However, the 200 examples of the XR 750 required for homologation could not be built in time for the 1969 season, so Harley-Davidson was only able to join in the racing scene again in 1970 – the year when Honda carried off its first racing victory. Besides the advent of the Japanese as serious competitors on the racetrack, there were other factors that led to the ground slipping from beneath Harley-Davidson in the racing business. Even the motorcycle sports umbrella organization, the AMA, which was strongly influenced by Harley-Davidson, was losing power because many racing motorcyclists were opposed to its sports politics. For example, the AMA continued to make a stand against road racing, which was becoming

From 1969 to 1981, Harley-Davidson belonged to the AMF group. The AMF logo did not develop into a symbol of quality ...

increasingly popular and which was mainly dominated by riders of foreign motorcycles. It banned sportsmen who took part in these races from entering AMA events. The AMA's biased attitude became increasingly evident, with the result that many clubs resigned from the AMA and many racing motorcyclists joined new organizations.

Meanwhile, the research and development department was busy increasing the specification of the Shovelhead and making it more attractive. Due to the increase in output compared to the Panhead, old problems long since thought to have been overcome were reappearing, such as vibration damage and symptoms of overheating. Alongside this project, new models were being worked on: in 1970, two middle-of-the-range motorcycles were introduced that had been developed at Aermacchi. The SS 350 road machine and the SX 350 scrambler both had single-cylinder engines, and the latter also had a high exhaust and knobbly tires. In the fall of the same year, a new model was finally presented for the 1971 season that found favor not only with Harley-Davidson's regular customers, but also with the fans of custom bikes who had until then been neglected. This machine was the FX 1200 Super Glide. The letters FX were derived from the F of the FLH

Electra Glide and the X of the XLH Sportster, and the machine itself was a cross between the two previous models, namely a stripped big twin with the telescopic forks and front wheel of the Sportster, without electric starter and with footpegs instead of footboards. The new model was the brainchild of William G. Davidson, who worked in the design department. A man of artistic sensitivity but with considerable technical know-how, he was a friendly, sociable type who was open-minded about modern bikers. With AMF's agreement, Willie G., as his friends called him, hung around in leathers and jeans at biker meetings and races, making direct contact with customers and target groups that had long been neglected. He knew what American motorcyclists were thinking and feeling, and as one of them he was familiar with the kind of motorbikes they wanted. The Super Glide was a success, and gave rise not only to a whole FX series, but also to the term "factory custom." The new style was also evident in Harley-Davidson's advertising language, which referred to the V-twin as the "All American Freedom Machine."

One year after the Super Glide, the two Sportster models were completely revised and launched onto the market with 1000cc engines: the XLCH 1000 as a sportier version, the XLH 1000 with

electric starter oriented partly towards touring, but more clearly contrasted with the FLH 1200 Electra Glide than before. Once again it had a hydraulic braking system and a front disc brake to cope with the weight of the dresser, which had risen steadily over the years.

Harley-Davidson offered racing motorcyclists two different versions of the XR 750, one for dirt-track racing and a version with fairing for racing on asphalt. Attention was drawn to the motorcycle outside the world of racing when stunt rider Robert "Evel" Knievel and his XR hit the headlines following some spectacular stunts. However, after his jump across Snake River Canyon failed and he had been in trouble with the law several times, Harley-Davidson stopped cooperating with Knievel.

During this time, some changes were made at Harley-Davidson, but they were not all for the better. Production at the Juneau Avenue plant was modernized relatively quickly and output was increased. However, modernization cost a large amount of money and this meant increasing prices. In the first year under AMF, there had already been three price rises, and both customers and dealers were annoyed about this. An Electra Glide now cost almost as much as a well-equipped Chevrolet Sedan. In addition, the care taken over assembly and quality control was suffering under the increased speed of

... either on the classic V-twin motorcycles or on the two-stroke singles such as the SS 125 (facing page) and the SS 250 (above).

production, and warranty claims were mounting at an alarming rate. The factory passed this problem on to dealers by placing the responsibility for final pre-delivery checks with the dealer who sold the machine. Only in particularly serious cases did the factory honor the warranty itself.

In addition to the exceptional strain placed on dealers, AMF now started a large clean-up campaign and sifted through the dealer network, looking for dealerships that did not fit the Harley-Davidson image. The assessment covered not only the condition and equipment of the shop and workshop, but also the neighborhood in which the dealership was located. Dealers who did not move or renovate their premises within a given period lost their contract.

Many dealers and customers were so annoyed about the new factory policy that they removed the AMF logo from machines that had been delivered to them – from 1971 onwards, this logo had been prominently displayed next to the Harley-Davidson badge on every motorcycle.

Even among the staff at Harley-Davidson, things did not always work out for the good of the company. A large proportion of the older, valued workers and salaried staff opted to take early retirement in view of the changes, and their experience was badly missed in Juneau Avenue. Discontent was also spreading among the

management because of interference from AMF's managers. However, before matters came to a head, Harley-Davidson sustained another shock. On August 23, 1971, William J. Harley died at the age of only 58 from chronic diabetes. The son of the company's founder, he was an enthusiastic motorcyclist and talented engineer, and as a young man he had worked his way up from the bottom in all areas of the factory. He had brought to his job as technical director immense experience, great practical ability and a high level of theoretical know-how. He was the father of the Sportster and had been awarded a medal by the Italian president for outstanding services to the Italian economy in his capacity as an Aermacchi director. Many who worked with him considered him the most capable heir of the company's founders and rated his loss to the factory correspondingly highly.

In the same year, Harley-Davidson lost another vice president: Walter Davidson Jr. left the company, stating as his reason that he no longer wished to be told what to do. He had worked for 21 years as general sales manager and successor to his uncle Arthur and was not entirely blameless for the company's problems, for he clung tenaciously to traditional marketing strategies. Nevertheless, his going was still a bitter loss. Harley-Davidson's production figures, which had been rocketing

upwards during this time – from only 30,000 units in 1970 to more than 70,000 in 1973 – disguised the fact that the company was still struggling with severe problems during the early 'seventies, and that AMF's managers had forced through a number of wrong decisions, resulting in dissatisfaction among dealers and customers alike. It is true that a new market had been opened up with the Super Glide, but growth at Harley-Davidson still could not keep pace with the gigantic boom in the entire motorcycle market, and the company's market share had dropped to well below six per cent in 1973. William H. Davidson realized that the company was in a dreadful state, and since he no longer wished to take responsibility as president for a company policy which was forced upon him, he resigned from his post on September 30, 1973 after being a company man for 45 years. AMF immediately appointed John H. O'Brien, a manager from its own ranks, to be the new president. Thus for the first time since it began, a man was at the head of the Harley-Davidson Motor Company who did not belong to either of the founding families. One of the first decisions he made was that part of the production was to be withdrawn from Milwaukee. When this plan was made known, the employees feared for their jobs and the trade unions called a strike.

1974
US president Richard M. Nixon resigns following the Watergate Affair, his successor is vice president Gerald Ford.

1975
The last US citizens leave Saigon; South Vietnam capitulates in the war against North Vietnam. *Apollo 19* docks successfully with the *Soviet Soyuz 18* spacecraft.

1976
Jimmy Carter wins the presidential elections in the USA. The American space probe *Viking II* lands on Mars.

1977
For the first time in 40 years, free elections are held in Spain. Elvis Presley and Charlie Chaplin die.

1978
Coup d'état by the army in Afghanistan, *rapprochement* with the Soviet Union. Sadat and Begin hold peace talks at Camp David.

1979
The Shah of Iran is overthrown, Ayatollah Khomeini assumes power. Radioactive gas escapes following an accident at Three Mile Island nuclear power station, Pennsylvania.

1980
Start of the war between Iran and Iraq. In New York, John Lennon is shot dead.

1981
IBM launches the personal computer (PC). Former film star Ronald Reagan becomes 40th president of the USA.

1982
War breaks out between Argentina and Great Britain over the Falkland Islands. Israel gives the Sinai Peninsula back to Egypt.

1983
US troops invade the Caribbean Island of Grenada. Soviet fighter planes shoot down a South Korean airliner with 269 on board; there are no survivors.

1974-1983

Extending the range and starting again

In 1973, in order to expand and further modernize production, and to avoid disputes with frustrated workers at the original factory, the AMF group spent millions converting an ammunition factory in York, Pennsylvania to the requirements of motorcycle production. A year later, the new Harley-Davidson president announced that important production sectors would be moving from Milwaukee to York. In future, only engines and transmissions would be produced in Milwaukee, plastic parts would continue to be made in Tomahawk, while chassis production and final assembly would be carried out in York. To this end, parts from Milwaukee and Tomahawk would be transported to York using the company's own trucks. However, the move in 1974 was ill-starred: hardly had production begun in

The FX 1200 Super Glide became increasingly popular as its styling imitated ever more closely that of the dealers and creators of customized motorcycles – this is the 1975 version. The term "factory custom" was coined, and the Super Glide became the forerunner of a whole series of FX customs.

After the success of the Super Glide, designed by Willie G. Davidson, AMF allowed him to design a sporty model: the XLCR 1000 Cafe Racer. The all-black Sportster special came onto the market in 1977, but was not a great success.

Also new in 1977 was the second model of the FX series, the FSX 1200 Low Rider, which was to become as successful and legendary as the Super Glide.

While Harley-Davidson continued to compete successfully in motorcycle sports – Jay Springsteen (above) was US champion in 1976, '77 and '78 – the model designers were concentrating on the custom series and created models like the Fat Bob of 1979 (left).

1978 was the year of the return to the 80 cubic inch (1340cc) engine. The gigantic motor was gradually fitted to all the FL and FX models, and in 1980 it was used for the FXS 80 Low Rider.

York than it was halted by a strike. The walk-out was only terminated three months later by substantial wage rises. The oil crisis also caused transport costs to escalate to unforeseen heights, rendering the original calculations useless. Only full use of the production capacity and further price increases could now maintain the company's profitability, and neither of these measures benefited either the quality or the competitiveness of the motorcycles.

The extremely high cost of spares increased the problems with suppliers of imitation parts, whose business was flourishing as never before. Also, competition from the Japanese motorcycle manufacturers was becoming increasingly serious. They were constantly introducing bigger and better models, and customers who would have bought an Electra Glide were now going for the Honda Gold Wing. Even the highway patrols, who had traditionally always been equipped with Harley-Davidsons, were now ordering Kawasakis, because the Japanese motorcycles were faster, cheaper, more reliable and easier to

During the 'sixties and 'seventies there were always two Sportster models: the XLH and XLCH. However, in 1978 the more sporty XLCH was discontinued, and for one year there was – as in the 'fifties – just one Sportster, "the one and only."

maintain. Honda and Kawasaki even set up production plants in the USA in order to avoid import restrictions.

Harley-Davidson's many problems prevented it from bringing new models onto the market. In 1974, only a Super Glide version with electric starter, known as the FXE, was introduced alongside the FX 1200. With a range of only five V-twins and a few unpopular, small, Italian-made bikes, Harley-Davidson could not survive in the hotly-contested market, and sales figures dropped again slightly after the rapid rise. In 1976, only 61,000 units were produced, and the limited anniversary edition launched in honor of the USA's bicentennial celebrations could not change this. That same year another member of the founding families, John E. Harley, died of cancer at the age of 61. By 1977, the number of motorcycles produced had dropped as low as 45,000. If William G. Davidson had not had the idea of the Super Glide, which had meanwhile come to resemble even more closely the usual custom bikes seen on the streets, this figure would certainly have been even lower.

Following the Super Glide's acceptance on the market, the company's management gave Willie G. the go-ahead in 1977 for two further very spirited models, the Cafe Racer, which was related to the Sportster, and the Low Rider, which was derived from the Super Glide. However, the fairly sporty, all-black Cafe Racer with cast alloy wheels, known as the XLCR 1000, was not received particularly well either by traditional Harley-Davidson customers or by other groups of motorcyclists. Only 3000 units were sold in two years, so it was removed from the range. On the other hand, the FXS 1200 Low Rider, also with alloy wheels, but with an extremely low seat and adhering even more closely in its details to custom styling than the Super Glide, was extremely popular with bikers.

For this reason, Harley-Davidson's research and development department continued to press AMF's management for the money to modernize the V-twin and extend the range. The success of the Super Glide and the Low Rider proved that there was profit to be made from satisfying the particular wishes of this target group.

As a pre-condition for further investment, AMF first sold Aermacchi to the Italian Cagiva group in 1978. It had been shown

that the sporting successes of this marque – Italian Walter Villa became world champion of the 250cc class on an Aermacchi-Harley-Davidson three times in a row – cost a lot of money, but had neither a positive effect on the sale of small two-stroke machines nor boosted sales of the big four-stroke machines. The fact that Harley-Davidson was able to win the US championships again on a regular basis with the XR 750, after its initial starting problems had been overcome – in 1975 with Gary Scott, in 1976, 1977 and 1978 with Jay Springsteen – carried more advertising weight in the USA than a world championship title.

After the sale of Aermacchi, Ray Albert Tritten, chairman of the board of AMF, agreed to further development work. That same year, as a temporary solution, the bore of the V-twin was enlarged to 80 cubic inches (1340cc), and this engine was then offered as an alternative to the 1200cc for the Electra Glide. The positive reaction to the Low Rider encouraged Harley-Davidson to make a policy of extending the range, and from then on it introduced new motorcycles annually. In 1979, at least one new model was introduced into each of the three series. To the dressers was added an even more luxuriously equipped FLHC 80 Electra Glide

One of Harley-Davidson's most consistently styled custom models is the FXWG 80 Wide Glide of 1980.

The FXB 80 Sturgis – here the '82 model – was named after the Black Hill Motorcycle Classic, an annual rally at Sturgis, South Dakota.

The Harley-Davidson FLT 80 Tour Glide was introduced in 1980 as a variant of the Electra Glide – here the Classic model, the FLTC 80 of 1982.

Classic – the two existing Electra Glide versions already came generously equipped with bar-mounted fairing, panniers and various accessories for the rider's comfort. In the custom series, the Super Glide and Low Rider were joined by the FXEF 1200 Fat Bob and and the FXWG 1200 Wide Glide. In the Sportster class, the XLCH 1000 without electric starter was withdrawn and the XLS Roadster 1000 introduced instead, a somewhat more comfortably tuned and equipped version of the XLH Sportster.

One year later, even the Low Rider, Fat Bob and Wide Glide were given the 80 cubic inch engine, and new bikes were added to the custom and dresser series – the 80 Sturgis and the FLT 80 Tour Glide. Erik Buell, a young engineer in the fully revived research and development department, was responsible for both models. The Sturgis was the first machine to be fitted as standard with toothed belts for the primary drive from the engine to the transmission and also for the secondary drive from the transmission to the rear wheel. For decades, roller chains had been used for this purpose, and some suppliers of accessories had already been in the habit of offering Harley-Davidson owners toothed belts so that they could upgrade their machines. Toothed belts were said to be more flexible, cause less noise and last longer. The Tour Glide was the more modern alternative to the Electra Glide: its fairing was frame-mounted, making the motorcycle more stable at high speeds; its engine was mounted in the frame using rubber components so that the driver and pillion passenger did not feel the vibrations as much; its ingeniously devised frame geometry promised improved handling; and the last gear of its five-speed transmission was designed as an overdrive so that the engine could run at 3000 rpm at highway speeds, thus reducing vibration and making the bike quieter and more economical.

Although AMF had agreed to the development of the new models, nobody in the group really believed that Harley-Davidson was going to recover. AMF's managers had hoped to participate in the motorcycle market boom when they purchased Harley-Davidson, but they underestimated both the problems in the company and the pressure of competition from Japanese manufacturers. It even seemed impossible to those in authority at AMF that they

In June 1981, the new owners of Harley-Davidson pose for the photographer – they are all company managers who have bought back "their" company from AMF with borrowed money.

would recover their investments in the form of profit, so they started looking for a buyer for Harley-Davidson as early as the mid 1970s.

In view of the completely changed world market for leisure goods, AMF's management decided at the end of the 'seventies to move the main emphasis of the product range from leisure to heavy industry. Harley-Davidson did not fit into this scheme at all, and AMF finally decided to sell the company. AMF's boss, Ray Albert Tritten, therefore appointed Vaughn Beals as a new Harley-Davidson director. He had the task of either finding a buyer or some other way of ridding AMF of its unloved motorcycle division.

Beals, an arts graduate and qualified engineer, but not necessarily a motorcycle fan at the start, astonishingly made it his ambition to save Harley-Davidson. He soon came to the conclusion that the marque would have the best chance of survival if it was split off from the AMF group and had to stand on its own feet again. This solution was discussed at numerous meetings and, in February 1981, a group of Harley-Davidson managers got together who were prepared to buy their company and

continue to run it. Among them was Vaughn Beals himself.

AMF agreed to the suggestion, asked approximately 80 million dollars for its share of Harley-Davidson and renounced its claims to factory buildings and machines in order to speed up the sale. The managers found a consortium of four banks which were prepared to put up the money, and each of the managers had to stand surety with up to 150,000 dollars of personal capital. On June 1, 1981 the transaction was complete, and the AMF chapter was closed for Harley-Davidson. The new owners were Vaughn Beals, Charles Thompson, William G. Davidson, John Hamilton, Dr. Jeffrey Bleustein, Kurt Woerpel, Chris Sartalis, James Paterson, Timothy Hoelter, David Lickerman, Peter Profumo, David Caruso and Ralph Swenson.

The AMF period has been interpreted very controversially with hindsight by various experts, and opinions as to where Harley-Davidson would be today without the AMF interlude vary widely. I am inclined to assume that AMF's injection of finance which the group finally had to write off as a loss – and was also in a position to write off because of its size and good economic state of health – enabled the Harley-Davidson company at least to survive – even if AMF's influence was not always based on a sound knowledge of motorcycles and finally left Harley-Davidson with serious quality and image problems. The fact remains that in 1969 AMF took over a

In 1982, Harley-Davidson tried to make entry into the range easier by introducing a particularly reasonably priced one-seater Sportster version, the XLX 61.

company with a management that had got stuck in a rut, working according to traditional methods and with an outdated production based on craftsman's skills. After nearly 12 years, AMF let go a company with a knowledgeable, committed management and relatively modern production plants. It is doubtful whether Harley-Davidson would ever have catered for the custom bike market under the old management and brought out such models as the Super Glide and Low Rider -- measures without which the company would never have survived.

The new Harley-Davidson company was split in 1981 into three divisions: Harley-Davidson Milwaukee in Wisconsin, Harley-Davidson York in Pennsylvania and Harley-Davidson International in Connecticut as the export division. Vaughn Beals became chairman of the board of directors and Charles Thompson was elected president. Beals saw the advantage of the newly created company as lying in the fact that it was being supported and guided by people for whom the Harley-Davidson marque had special meaning, and who would therefore give everything to see it achieve success. To emphasize this, an advertising campaign was launched with the motto "motorcycles by the people for the people." The return to the old headquarters and the new beginning for the Harley-Davidson marque was celebrated by the new company management with a joint motorcycle ride from York to Milwaukee. Then

the outlines of the new company policy were announced: modernization of the existing models, expansion of the model range, cooperative relationship with dealers and aggressive action against companies that dealt in Harley-Davidson motorcycles and parts without authorization, or that had original parts copied in Taiwan, Korea and Japan in order to sell them at rock-bottom prices in the USA. In early 1982, Harley-Davidson began legal proceedings against these suppliers ·of aftermarket parts. When this process became too long drawn out, Harley-Davidson made a stand by offering its customers, in addition to the original Wisconsin-made parts, cheaper accessories and spares under the name "Eagle Iron." These were made in the Far East, like the products sold by the aftermarket parts suppliers.

However, the economic climate for Harley-Davidson's new beginning was anything but favorable. The interest rate was more than 20 per cent, and this turned the company's finance arrangements into a balancing act. The oil crisis and federal mismanagement during the 1970s had led the USA into a deep recession which naturally resulted in the motorcycle market shrinking dramatically. This collapse of the

market, the extent of which could not have been foreseen, led to a ruinous price war among the Japanese motorcycle manufacturers, who hardly ever took back their machines once they had been imported, with the result that enormous stocks accumulated in the warehouses of importers and dealers. By the end of the 1981 financial year, the Japanese had sold about 800,000 motorcycles in the USA – as against Harley-Davidson's 30,000 – but by the fall of 1982 warehouse stocks had grown to 1.4 million units. Machines from the motorcycle mountain were frequently offered for sale at below cost price, just to avoid the enormous interest and storage costs. This development not only ruined many dealers, but also wiped out the market in second-hand motorcycles and robbed Harley-Davidson, now a small motorcycle manufacturer by world standards, of any competitive potential.

There was no sign that the situation was going to improve and, after Harley-Davidson had already had to make 200 employees redundant in the fall of 1981, mass redundancies became unavoidable in the spring of the following year. Some 1600 out of the staff of 3800 had to go, among them John Harley Jr., the last company member of the Harley family. Salaries were frozen and social welfare benefits reduced. In addition, the manufacturing rights for golf carts and industrial vehicles were sold off to a company in Ohio in order to free up some capital.

Vaughn Beals had to admit that the company was on the verge of bankruptcy, and he asked for help from the state in the form of an import restriction. Once before, in 1978, an attempt had failed to get the government to impose a general import restriction on foreign motorcycles. Nevertheless, Beals saw a renewed request as the last chance for Harley-Davidson. The situation had also worsened compared to 1978: the existence of the company and with it thousands of jobs in the factories and dealerships were now at risk. Many other American companies in the vehicle and electrical industries were also in the same boat. To increase his chances, Beals limited the request this time to motorcycles over 700cc, and the duration of the restrictions to five years, indicating that the debt-burdened company could regenerate itself in that time. This time, there was also a new American president, Ronald Reagan, who was said to be more concerned with protecting domestic industry than his predecessor, Jimmy Carter.

The hearings of the International Trade Commission took three weeks, then the request was granted. The Commission decided upon a drastic increase in the usual import duty of 4.4 per cent for motorcycles with high cubic capacity, followed by a step-by-step reduction over the next five years. The duty was to be set at 49.4 per cent the first year, 39.4 per cent the second, 29.4 per cent the third, 19.4 per cent the fourth and 14.4 per cent the fifth year, before dropping back to the original level in the sixth year. The

Japanese manufacturers were also to be granted increasing annual tax exemption limits: for the first year the limit was 6000 motorcycles, to be increased by a further 1000 each year. President Reagan signed the Trade Commission's draft, and the regulation came into force on April 15, 1982. All at once, Harley-Davidson had a breathing space and had gained a good measure of competitiveness.

Neither in Milwaukee nor in York did anyone sit back and relax. Important measures for increasing quality were introduced, new models launched and close contact with the customer sought. The assembly line production introduced

under AMF was dispensed with and the assembly line workers were reorganized into small groups who together assembled individual motorcycles. This made the work more interesting, and it was easier to see results. Employees were able to identify with the product they had created, and quality improved.

All three series were extended in 1982. The Sportster was completely revised for its 25th anniversary. It was given a new chassis that reduced the motorcycle's weight to below 500 lbs (230kg) and promised better handling. To the XL series was added the XLX 61, a particularly reasonably-priced one-seater model at about 4000 dollars, which was intended to make buying into the Harley-Davidson range easier. Nevertheless, the difference in price compared to Japanese motorcycles was still considerable – for the price of a Sportster you could buy two 750s from the Far East.

The FL series now comprised four models, for the Electra Glide and the Tour Glide were now available as luxuriously appointed Classic versions. Although the Tour Glide was clearly the more modern machine, the Electra Glide remained in the range because many dresser fans did not want to have to get used to the unaccustomed features of the newer model. The FXE Super Glide was the last of the big twins to get an 80 cubic inch engine, and was joined by its two future successors, the FXR and FXRS 80 Super Glide II, which primarily featured the flexible, vibration-damping engine mounting and a new five-speed transmission. The primary drive of the FXB 80 Sturgis introduced two years previously had in the meantime given rise to warranty claims, so the toothed belt was abandoned for the primary drive, but the FXS 80 Low Rider inherited the toothed belt for its secondary drive – thus one model was derived from two, namely the FXSB 80 Low Rider with roller chain as the primary drive and toothed belt as the secondary drive.

The 74 cubic inch version of the big twin had now finally disappeared, but in 1983 another interesting engine was introduced into the Harley-Davidson range. The XR 1000 as a road version of the XR 750 racing machine was added to the Sportster series, an extremely sporty model by Harley-Davidson standards and, at supposedly more than 70 hp, the most powerful and probably the fastest

In 1982 there were three Sportster models in the Harley-Davidson range – apart from the XLH and the XLX there was also the XLS Roadster 1000, pictured here, which was introduced in 1979 as a machine oriented more towards touring.

Likewise in 1982, the legendary Super Glide was joined by its later successor, the Super Glide II, the FXR 80 version of which was to be the forerunner of today's Super Glide, and the FXRS 80 version, pictured here, the forerunner of the Low Glide.

From 1983 a fourth model joined the Sportster series for a short time, namely the XR 1000, which was based on the works racing machine, the XR 750 – this new model was and still is the fastest standard Harley-Davidson of all time.

Also from 1983, the epitome of the classic Harley-Davidson: the Electra Glide – here the FLHC Classic model – already with the Evolution engine which was only readily available the following year.

standard Harley-Davidson that has ever been offered for sale. In contrast to the usual type of construction in which both cylinders were fitted with a single carburetor located in the V of the cylinder heads, the XR was fitted with two carburetors arranged at the back, whose eye-catching air filters could be a problem for the rider's right leg. After enormous interest from the dealers initially, the motorcycle did not sell as well as expected. Production was stopped, and it took until 1985 for all the stocks of the XR 1000 to be sold.

But 1983 was not only a year for new models. Harley-Davidson also founded the Harley Owners Group or HOG the same year. Every buyer of a Harley-Davidson automatically became a member and was entitled to the first year of membership free. Thereafter an annual

subscription of 30 dollars enabled the member to continue to take advantage of HOG's services. Among the benefits were a subscription to *The Enthusiast* magazine, assistance in case of accident or damage, and a constantly updated register of stolen Harley-Davidsons. By founding HOG, the company was attempting to revive the old feeling of belonging together that used to be prevalent among customers, dealers and Harley-Davidson employees.

Nearing completion at the end of this period in the company's history was the most important project of all – a project that was to have a decisive influence on Harley-Davidson's future and put an end to the loss-making phase that was still dragging on – the Evolution Engine was almost ready for production.

1984
The Indian prime minister Indira Gandhi is assassinated. Niki Lauda wins the Formula I World Championship for the third time.

1985
Michail Gorbachev becomes the new head of the Soviet Union. Compact discs and CD players begin competing against LPs and record players.

1986
In the Soviet Union, the nuclear power station at Chernobyl gets out of control. In the Philippines, President Marcos is overthrown.

1987
In the US, Congressional committees start investigating the Iran Contra affair.

1988
The Soviet Union withdraws after more than eight years' occupation of Afghanistan. Iran and Iraq call off their war in the Gulf.

1989
George Bush becomes 41st president of the USA. In Peking, more than 2000 demonstrators are butchered by Chinese military units in Tiananmen square.

1990
The GDR is dissolved and the first elections are held in a united Germany. Lithuania, Latvia and Estonia declare their independence.

1991
Six-week Gulf War between the allied troops of 31 UN nations and Iraq. Eleven former Soviet republics join together to form the CIS and dissolve the USSR.

1992
Civil war in the former Yugoslavia.

After 1983

The Evolution engine and the consolidation of the legend

In 1984, the last profound change to be made to the legendary Harley-Davidson V-twin engine was complete and the improved engine went into production. After seven years of development work, a new engine, known as the Evolution, replaced the Shovelhead. This latter engine had earned such a poor image during the AMF period due to problems with quality and the associated guarantee claims and maintenance difficulties that a thorough reworking and renaming of the V-twin was long overdue. The Evolution engine had new cylinders and cylinder heads, but the same crankcase as the Shovelhead and also worked with the same stroke-bore ratio. The newly designed pistons now had a flat crown which, along with the narrower valve angle, produced a more compact combustion chamber and enabled a higher compression to be achieved. The new engine weighed less than its predecessor, ran more smoothly, was thermally sounder and promised greater reliability and a longer working life. It was at first only fitted as an 80 cubic inch version in three models in the FL series, namely the Electra Glide Classic, the Tour Glide and the Tour Glide Classic. Mounted in the frame using rubber components in order to isolate the rider from vibrations, it transmitted its power to the rear wheel via a five-speed

Harley-Davidson blossomed again during the eighties thanks to the FX series – here the FXRS Low Glide of 1984 – and the new Evolution engine.

transmission and toothed belt instead of the roller chain which was customary on most models, but which required a certain amount of maintenance.

The year 1984 also saw three new models added to the FX series, the FXRS Low Glide as the successor to the FXRS Super Glide II, the FXRT Sport Glide and the FXST Softail, which were all fitted with the new engine and represented the logical continuation of the policy of extending the range that

Following on from the FLT Tour Glide, Harley-Davidson's second machine with frame-mounted fairing was also its second attempt to modernize the traditional design: the FXRT Sport Glide of 1984.

With the FXST Softail, Harley-Davidson succeeded in 1984 in combining the appearance of the solid rear end of the fifties with the comfortable suspension of the eighties: the telescopic arms are hidden underneath the engine.

had begun in the late 1970s. Above all, the Softail's design attracted attention. The front part of the motorcycle was based on the Wide Glide, but the back was reminiscent of the solid rear end of the pre-war period and early post-war years. The rear axle appeared to be solidly screwed onto the main frame – however the triangular rear frame section was in fact a three-dimensional swing arm which was supported against the

In 1984, the FL series consisted of four models: the FLHT Electra Glide, the FLHTC Electra Glide Classic (pictured here), the FLT Tour Glide and FLTC Tour Glide Classic. Only the Electra Glide was still powered by the Shovelhead, all the others had the Evolution engine.

The Tour Glide models – pictured here is the FLTC Tour Glide Classic of 1984 – have superior handling to the Electra Glides, but have not been able to force the two classic models out of the range.

The FXEF Fat Bob, which had been dropped in 1982, was given another lease of life in 1985 with the Evolution engine – only for one season, however, then it went out of production again, as did the FXWG Wide Glide.

From 1985 there was only one Super Glide again, the FXR powered by the Evolution engine – the FXE with the Shovelhead had been dropped the previous year, and the FXRS had become the Low Glide.

In 1985, the FLHT Electra Glide was the last member of the FL and FX families to be given the Evolution engine. Only the Sportster models had to wait another year for theirs.

frame on two horizontal telescopic arms hidden between the base bars of the frame underneath the engine, thus combining the forties look with the comfortable suspension of the eighties. The name "Softail" gave a clue, but you had to look closely to discover the secret of this model's apparently solid rear end.

In order to make the advantages of the new motorcycles known to the public as quickly as possible, Harley-Davidson introduced the "Super Ride" demonstration program. Demonstration models of the new motorcycles were available at all authorized dealers and at large American motorcycle meetings – a scheme which met with such a positive response that it became a regular feature.

That same year, Harley-Davidson won the Californian Highway Patrol Contract – for the first time in 10 years the motorcycles from Milwaukee came up to the strict criteria of the Californian highway police and were able to beat the Japanese competition fairly and squarely. The contract was renewed again and again in the years that followed, so that the number of Harley-Davidson police motorcycles on the Californian highways grew steadily.

From 1985, the Electra Glide, the Super Glide and the Low Rider were fitted with the Evolution engine. The Wide Glide was also given the new engine, but only for this one year, for it was so similar to the new Softail, apart from the rear wheel suspension, that it could not be kept in the range for very much longer. 1985 was also the last production year for the Fat Bob, which had been dropped three years previously and had now been brought back to life for a short time with the Evolution engine, while the FXRS Low Glide had been virtually merged with the FXSB Low Rider. Both models lived on in the FXRS Low Rider.

The 1985 models received a special award from two trade unions, the AIW (Allied Industrial Workers of America) and the IAM (International Association of Machinists and Aerospace Workers), which were responsible for representing the Harley-Davidson staff. With this seal of quality, the workers wanted to emphasize – so the union representative said – that they had done everything they could for the products and wanted to express to the consumer their complete faith in them.

With the Evolution engine, Harley-Davidson very quickly won back customer confidence. Despite the shrinking motorcycle market worldwide, the company was able to increase its output year by year and return to making a profit.

By 1986 the process was complete: the development of the small Evolution engine for the XL series was finished and the new Sportster came onto the market as an 883cc one-seater introductory model to the range.

For more demanding customers, Harley-Davidson introduced the XLH Sportster 1100 in 1986. This not only had a larger cubic capacity than the basic Sportster but offered a pillion seat and superior equipment.

Even so, 1985 was a year of looming crisis because the leading bank of the four which had financed the buying out of the company from AMF wanted to pull out and claim back its loan. However, the head of finance, Rich Teerlink, succeeded in finding someone else to put up the money and in negotiating a refinancing plan with him by that December. This put the company on such a firm footing that it was able to issue shares again the following year. In July 1986, Harley-Davidson was able to offer two million preference shares totaling 20 million

1986 was also a year of important new models for the custom series. One of these was the Sport Edition of the Low Rider, which satisfied the demands of the sportier-minded Harley-Davidson riders with its two disc brakes on the front wheel and increased road clearance when cornering.

The second new model for 1986 in the FX series was the Grand Touring Edition of the FXRT Sport Glide. However, it only remained in production for one year.

Also in 1986, Willie G. Davidson thought up a new styling idea, the FXSTC Softail Custom with rear disc wheel – thus following even more closely the customization trend within the standard range.

In 1987, Harley-Davidson introduced as an alternative to the one-seater XLH Sportster 883 a de luxe version with dual seat and spoke wheels.

Custom bikes continued to be the accepted thing in Milwaukee: in 1987 the FXLR Low Rider Custom was introduced – like the Softail Custom it was also fitted with a rear disc wheel.

dollars as well as non-voting share certificates to the value of 70 million dollars. Having learnt from the experience with AMF, Harley-Davidson managers incorporated a number of clauses in the statutes of the new joint-stock company which were designed to prevent the take-over of the company simply by a majority shareholding. These clauses have worked right up to the present day, although Harley-Davidson shares have developed into securities that are not merely bought for sentimental reasons. Who would have thought in 1986 that their price would have increased tenfold by the end of 1991? The improving economic situation also enabled Harley-Davidson to buy the Holiday Rambler Corporation, a manufacturer of leisure vehicles – camper vans and caravans – as well as special commercial products such as small trucks and rescue vehicles.

As a thoroughly American company, Harley-Davidson also had to make a contribution towards the 1986 celebrations marking the 100th birthday of the Statue of Liberty in New York. To celebrate the anniversary, special "Liberty Edition" models were created and 100 dollars for every model sold were given to the Ellis Island Foundation for renovating the statue. In this way, 250,000 dollars was raised, which Vaughn Beals symbolically handed over to the foundation at the end of the "Ride of Liberty," a rally in which Beals led thousands of Harley-Davidson riders right across the northern half of the USA from west to east and Willie G. Davidson led a second, equally large, group through the southern part of the country. All met up in Washington DC and rode together to Liberty State Park, New Jersey, for the final ceremony.

It was also in 1986 that the Sportster series was renovated. The old 1000cc engine went out of production, and with it the XLX, Roadster and XR models, but the Sportster was revised and given an Evolution engine, with a choice of 883 or 1100cc. The new engine, made from light metals, had now also found its way into the XL series. Harley-Davidson was thus fitting all the machines in its range with Evolution engines, and now also had a model in the attractive class of under 1000cc – at a thoroughly competitive price. A Sportster 883 cost 3995 dollars at the time of its introduction – 800 dollars less than the Sportster 1000 of the previous year. Like most Harley-Davidson models in the meantime, the Sportsters were now available with cast alloy wheels as standard instead of spoke wheels. While in the past spoke wheels were the standard and cast alloy wheels the exception, the opposite was to be the case in future. That same year Harley-Davidson introduced to the market a custom version of the Softail with a rear disc wheel, and a sport edition of the Low Rider with a double disc brake in front and more road clearance to allow for a sporty riding style. However, the design sensation of 1986 was a motorcycle introduced for the following season, the FLST Heritage Softail which, with its enclosed telescopic forks, bulky fenders and apparently rigid rear end, already familiar from the FXST Softail, was the spitting image of the Hydra Glide of 1949. With the Heritage, the Softail rear suspension had now also found its way into the FL series. A new type of motorcycle had thus come into being, which could be called a retrobike – modern technology in the style of the good old days.

The following year, Harley-Davidson had a new idea concerning sales strategy for the American market that would further the role of the Sportster as an entry level bike to the range. Anyone who purchased a Sportster 883 from new and traded it in within two years in part exchange for a model from the FX or FL series would get the full purchase price of the 883 deducted by the dealer from the price of the new bike. This tempting offer was made even more attractive by the fact that three new 1340cc models for the coming year were presented in 1987: firstly, the Classic version of the Heritage Softail, the FLSTC, with windshield and studded leather panniers; secondly, the FLHS Electra Glide Sport, a slimmed-down version of the Electra Glide that came very close, with its 'fifties charm, to the latter machine; and thirdly, on the occasion of the tenth birthday of the Low Rider, a custom model of the same with forged handlebars, rear disc wheel and front spoke wheel.

However, the news item which attracted most attention that year was when Harley-Davidson asked the International Trade Commission to lift prematurely the import restrictions on motorcycles that it had introduced four years previously at the company's request. This was a unique action, for never before had an

The most important new model of 1987: the FLST Heritage Softail – with its 'fifties styling it was the first retrobike, and with its apparently solid rear end it was the first Softail model in the FL series.

A fourth model was added to the XL series in 1988: the XLH Sportster Hugger 883 with high buckhorn handlebars and spoke wheels.

Also in 1988, the big Sportster's cubic capacity was increased from 1100 to 1200cc, and the bike was known from then on as the XLH Sportster 1200.

The FXSTS Springer Softail, and its revival of the Springer front forks that had been abandoned in the 'fifties, caused just as much of a stir in 1988 as the Heritage Softail had done the previous year.

Just one year after the introduction of the Heritage Softail, it was joined in 1988 by a Classic version with windshield and studded leather panniers that was known as the FLSTC.

The last model to be introduced in 1988 was a slimmed-down version of the Electra Glide, known as the FLHS Electra Glide Sport.

Enough is never enough: in 1989, the Super Tourer FLHTC Electra Glide Classic was supplemented by the even more luxurious FLHTU Electra Glide Ultra Classic (below).

American company asked for restrictive measures against its competitors to be terminated. This step was evidence of the company's new self-confidence – Harley-Davidson was once again market leader in the USA for motorcycles over 850cc – and it also demonstrated a flair for public relations. For the price of state protection, which was soon to run out anyway, Harley-Davidson gave proof of its competitiveness worldwide.

It was like another present when Ronald Reagan delivered a highly personal message to Harley-Davidson. The American president was visiting the York factory, at the invitation of Vaughn Beals, when he expressed to staff and management his respect for the achievement of the last few years. He then pressed the starter button on a Sportster 1100 as it rolled off the assembly line, making it spring to life.

At the end of the year, Harley-Davidson acquired from the British company Armstrong the worldwide rights to the MT 500 all-terrain military motorcycle, which was equipped with a single-cylinder four-stroke engine from the Austrian company

Rotax. This was a further step taken by Harley-Davidson with a view to widening its scope of activity beyond classic V-twin motorcycles.

In 1988 there were two further innovations worthy of note in addition to the motorcycles already mentioned. Firstly, the cubic capacity of the large Sportster was increased to 1200cc. This made it the Sportster with the largest cubic capacity of all time. The XL series now consisted of four models, for the one-seater 883 standard version had been joined by a Hugger with higher handlebars and a two-seater De Luxe version. Secondly, on the occasion of the company's 85th birthday, a form of front wheel suspension was revived which Bill Harley had developed in 1906 for the "Silent Gray Fellow," and that had been abandoned in the 1950s, namely the Springer fork. It may have looked antiquated by 1980s standards, but it had been completely revised and – as its use in practice proved – it was just as effective as the conventional telescopic fork. The model chosen to receive the Springer fork was none other than a Softail – christened the Springer Softail. This

Harley-Davidson also brought out a luxury version of the Tour Glide in 1989: the FLTU Tour Glide Ultra Classic – the picture shows the '93 model.

There has been an FXRS Low Rider Convertible since 1990 for fans of the Low Rider who can't make up their minds: take off the touring accessories such as the windshield and panniers, and you've got the Sport Edition.

With the introduction in 1990 of the FLSTF Fat Boy, the barriers finally came down between the customs and dressers: the Fat Boy not only had a Softail, it also counted as a genuine custom bike despite the letters FL.

Harley-Davidson is always on the lookout for new lines – it acquired the rights to the MT 500 military motorcycle made by the British company Armstrong, which is powered by an Austrian Rotax engine. The picture shows a 1990 model.

Even in the 'nineties, Harley-Davidson technology still wins world records, as proven by the 322 mph land speed record of 1990.

In 1991, the first model of a new group in the FX series was launched as a limited edition – the FXDB Dyna Glide Sturgis.

In 1992, as planned, the Sturgis was replaced by the FXDB Dyna Glide Daytona (shown here) and the FXDC Dyna Glide Custom – once again only for one season.

motorcycle, the FXSTS, made just as nostalgic an impression with its combination of (apparently) unsprung rear wheel and (genuine) Springer front forks as the Heritage Softail, even if there was no immediate similarity to an earlier model.

Harley-Davidson used the company's 85th anniversary as an excuse for another mass ride, and at the same time attempted to correct the public image of the Harley-Davidson rider, which still had negative associations because outlaws principally rode Harley-Davidsons. The general public was unaware that this group only accounted for a very small proportion of the Harley-Davidson community, and it did not help either that an outsider could not tell the difference, going on outward appearance alone, between many of the free bikers and the one per cent of outlaws. What would therefore be more obvious than to dedicate the ride to a good cause? The event was used to collect money for the Muscular Dystrophy Association, and the motto was "Motorcyclists fight against muscular dystrophy." Participants assembled at ten different locations in the USA, and in the end more than 35,000 Harley-Davidson riders set off for Milwaukee. They collected a total of 600,000 dollars for the good cause. Harley-Davidson's successful PR measures also had an effect on the presidential campaign. Both candidates, the Republican George Bush and the Democrat Michael Dukakis, mentioned the company in their speeches as being a successful and exemplary American enterprise. Meanwhile, elections were also being held at Harley-Davidson: Richard F. Teerlink was elected as the new president of Harley-Davidson Inc., and James H. Paterson as president of the motorcycle division.

In the last months of 1988, the research and development department was paying particular attention to the FL series, which was fitted in 1989 with a more powerful alternator and a computer-controlled turn signal cancelling mechanism. To the luxury touring machines, the Electra Glide Classic and Tour Glide Classic, was added a still more extravagantly equipped model, the Ultra Classic.

The following year, Harley-Davidson intensified its efforts to fulfil the individual wishes of as many customers as possible, and brought two more new models onto the market: the FLSTF Fat Boy, derived from the Heritage Softail but with disc wheels and a few changes to details such as a new exhaust, and the FXRS Low Rider Convertible, which was intended to combine two models in one – if you take off the windshield and panniers which make touring with the motorcycle more pleasurable, you have the sport edition of the Low Rider.

The policy of continuing to extend the range was proving successful: in 1990, for the fifth year running, Harley-Davidson was the leader in the American motorcycle market for machines over 850cc. Its market share was 62.3 per cent and well ahead of the nearest competitor, Honda, at 16.2 per cent. Even developments on foreign markets more than satisfied Harley-Davidson managers, for since 1985 the trend had been consistently upwards. In 1985, 5619 motorcycles were exported and a total of 34,815 produced, and the figures for 1990 were 62,458 units produced, of which 19,320 were exported.

In 1990 and 1991 there were two anniversaries in the USA which affected Harley-Davidson indirectly. In August 1990, in the small town of Sturgis in South Dakota, thousands of motorcyclists, mostly on Harley-Davidsons, gathered for the 50th Black Hills Motorcycle Classic. The Bike Week at Daytona Beach, Florida, celebrated the same anniversary in March 1991. The real reason for this event, which is also primarily attended by Harley-Davidson riders, is the 200 mile race together with supporting program at the Daytona Speedway. However, the majority of the countless visitors don't have much to do with the racing, their motto being "to hell with the races, I came to party." On the occasion of each of these anniversaries, Harley-Davidson brought out a special model which was presented at the particular gathering and sold during the following season.

There had already been a Sturgis in 1981/82, a version of the Low Rider, and

Once again, two Harley-Davidson model groups, namely Dyna Glide and Low Rider, were linked with the introduction of the '93 FXDL Dyna Glide Low Rider.

The '93 FLSTN Heritage Softail Nostalgia with whitewall tires and cowhide trim on panniers and seat was already presented in the spring of 1992 at the Daytona Bike Week.

Also new for 1993 and a revival of the FXWG Wide Glide, which went out of production in 1985, was the Harley-Davidson FXDWG Dyna Wide Glide.

the appearance of the black-painted anniversary model was naturally based on this. However, the frame, the engine mounting and many details were completely new, so that the '91 Sturgis counted in fact as a new model by the name of FXDB Dyna Glide. The next year, the Sturgis was followed for another year under the same model code by the ochre-colored Daytona and, because the Dyna Glide principle was so popular, by the silver FXDC Dyna Glide Custom.

Harley-Davidson continued the tradition of presenting in March each year the model for the following season – almost twelve months in advance – at the 1992 Bike Week. At Daytona Beach, the FLSTN Heritage Softail Nostalgia was already to be seen, a variation of the Heritage Softail Classic with white-walled tires and real cow hide trim on the seat and leather panniers. The Nostalgia was followed for the 1993 anniversary year, in which Harley-Davidson celebrated the company's 90 years of existence, by two further models from the Dyna Glide series, namely the FXDL Dyna Glide Low Rider and the FXDWG Dyna Wide Glide, as well as limited anniversary versions of six different models and belt drive for all Sportster models.

Are you completely bewildered now by all these model codes and names? It's hardly surprising, since Harley-Davidson currently has about 20 models on the market. To help you keep track, over the page you will find a summary of the engines from the various periods from the De Dion engine with atmospheric valve to the Evolution engine. There also follows a family tree which covers the 90-year history of Harley-Davidson, listing both the singles of the early days and the V-twin models from the first 61s up to the current model range. This will help you to see when each model was introduced and when it was taken out of production, which motorcycle was fitted with which engine, and which machine belonged to which series. If you then compare the family tree with the photos of the models in the book and re-read the text here and there, you will soon become an expert on Harley-Davidson.

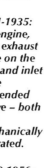

1903-1910: De Dion engine with atmospherically controlled inlet valve.

1911-1935: ioe engine, with exhaust valve on the side and inlet valve suspended above – both now mechanically operated.

1929-1956: side-valve engine with inlet and exhaust valves positioned next to each other, also called the Flathead.

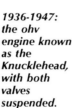

1936-1947: the ohv engine known as the Knucklehead, with both valves suspended.

1948-1965: the ohv engine christened the Panhead, with hydraulic lifters.

1966-1985: the ohv engine of the big twins, known as the Shovelhead.

From 1984: all-aluminum ohv engine known as the Evolution engine.

The different types of engine

The Harley-Davidson V-twin can confidently be called a milestone in the history of technology because it has been in continuous production longer than any other internal-combustion engine. Since its introduction in 1909, the principle of operation, number and arrangement of cylinders, cooling system and number of valves have not changed – it was always an air-cooled four-stroke two-cylinder V engine with two valves per cylinder. In principle, all that changed during its first 20 years was the method of valve operation. However, since 1936 the engine has also remained unchanged in this respect and only small details have been refined.

It began in 1909 with the De Dion principle: the exhaust valve was situated on the side of the cylinder and was operated by a camshaft below it, while the inlet valve in the cylinder head was atmospherically controlled. Atmospherically controlled means that the snifting valve, as it is also known, opens of its own accord when there is a partial vacuum in the combustion chamber, and it closes when the pressure there is greater than normal atmospheric pressure.

However, Harley-Davidson soon saw the need for a mechanically operated inlet valve, and something was done about it as early as 1911. The camshaft was also made to operate the inlet valve, which remained in the cylinder head, via rods and levers. The inlet valve was thus positioned above the exhaust valve that was located on the side of the cylinder, and this principle of valve operation became known as "inlet over exhaust" or "ioe."

The ioe system was retained by Harley-Davidson for the V-twin for a very long time. Only in 1929 was the 45 cubic inch little twin brought out with a system that was very popular in the automobile industry, and very easy to maintain, in which both valves were positioned on the side of the cylinder. This system was known as the "side-valve" or "sv." It was also adopted one year later for the 74 cubic inch engine. Since such an engine needs nothing other than a flat lid for a cylinder head, it was also referred to as a "Flathead" in the automobile industry. Even though the cylinder heads of the air-cooled Harley-Davidson engines did not look as flat because of their cooling fins, the term was also adopted for these side-valve motorcycle engines.

The 61 cubic inch engine was first changed in 1936, when it bypassed the side valves and was fitted with overhead valves, the abbreviation for this system being "ohv." With this system, both valves hang in the cylinder head and are operated by the camshaft, which is still positioned underneath, via lifters, push rods and rocker arms. Such a valve mechanism naturally makes for a larger cylinder head – because it has to house the valves as well – and generally one or more cylinder head covers which give access to the parts inside the head.

As engine technology advanced, other designs followed the ohv, using an overhead camshaft (ohc) or double overhead camshafts (dohc), with four, five or even eight valves per cylinder. However, Harley-Davidson has kept to the ohv two-valve engine right up to the present day, and customers differentiate between the various generations of engine according to the shape of the cylinder head or the cylinder head cover. The head of the big twin that was introduced in 1936 reminded fans of the knuckles of a fist, and therefore became known as the "Knucklehead." In 1948, a generation of engines followed in the big twins whose cylinder head covers, with a little imagination, were reminiscent of overturned cake-pans, and so were known as "Panheads." Eighteen years later, in 1966, there followed the "Shovelhead," whose cover – as you can guess – looked like an overturned coal shovel blade. Finally, in 1984, the big twins of the dresser and custom lines, and two years later the little twin of the Sportsters, were given the last version of the V-twin to date, the "Evolution engine." It was given this name officially by the factory, and then also by the customers, who were obviously unable to think of a nickname this time.

In the case of the little twin, there was only one generation of engines between the side-valve design and the Evolution engine, so no differentiation was made here between Knuckleheads, Panheads and Shovelheads.

Continued on page 76   Continued on page 76   Continued on page 76

The Harley-Davidson Family Tree 1903-1934

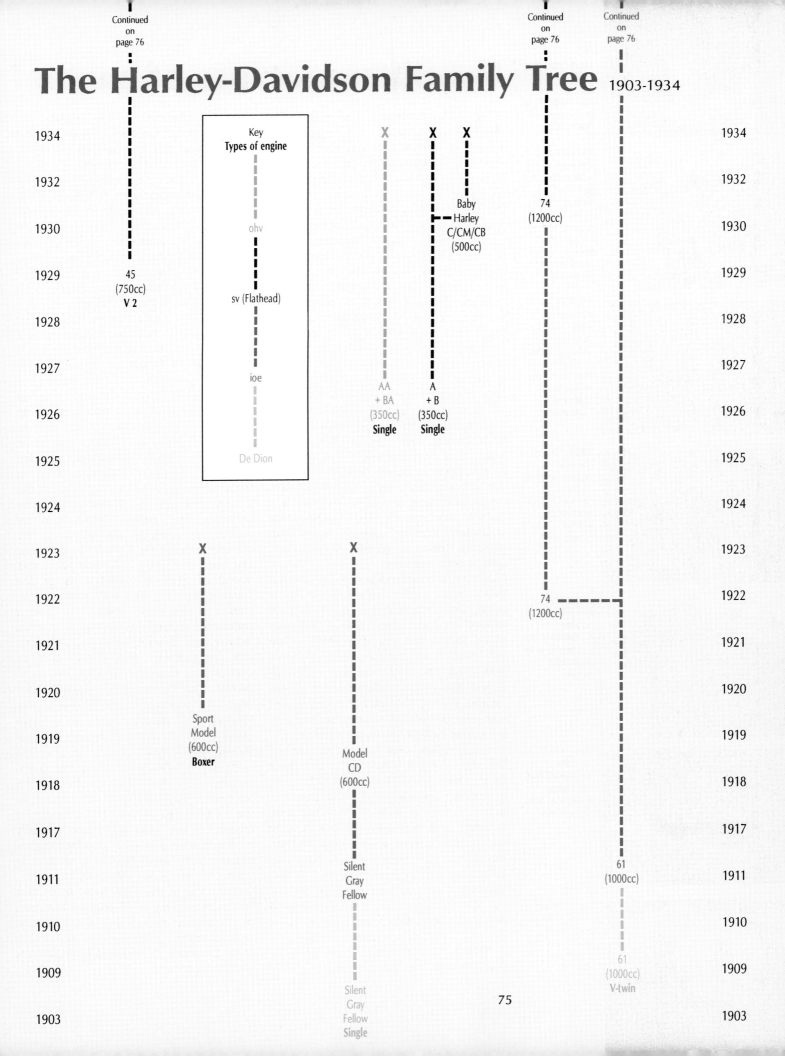

Key
Types of engine

ohv

sv (Flathead)

ioe

De Dion

1934

1932

1930

1929 — 45 (750cc) **V 2**

1928

1927

1926

1925

1924

1923

1922

1921

1920

1919 — Sport Model (600cc) **Boxer**

1918 — Model CD (600cc)

1917

1911 — Silent Gray Fellow

1910

1909 — 61 (1000cc) V-twin

1903 — Silent Gray Fellow **Single**

X — AA + BA (350cc) **Single**

X — A + B (350cc) **Single**

X — Baby Harley C/CM/CB (500cc)

74 (1200cc)

74 (1200cc)

61 (1000cc)

75

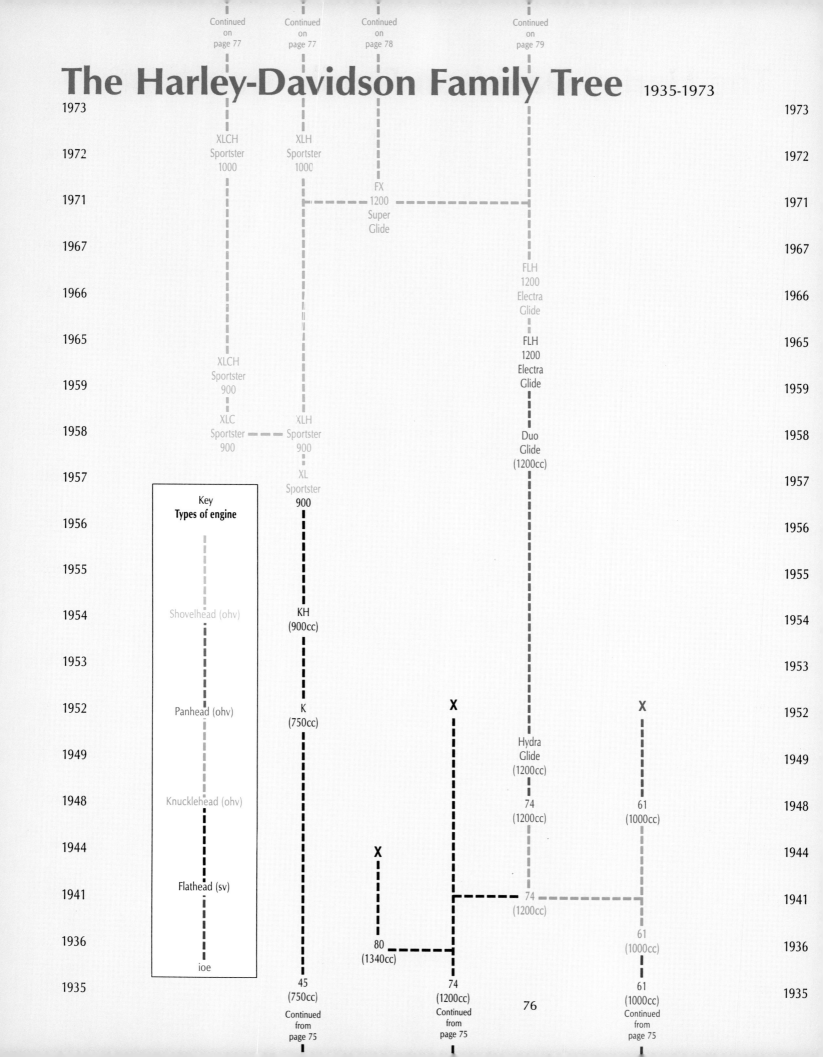

The Harley-Davidson Family Tree 1935-1973

Continued on page 77

Continued on page 77

Continued on page 78

Continued on page 79

1973

1972 — XLCH Sportster 1000 — XLH Sportster 1000

1971 — FX 1200 Super Glide

1967

1966 — FLH 1200 Electra Glide

1965 — FLH 1200 Electra Glide

1959 — XLCH Sportster 900

1958 — XLC Sportster 900 — XLH Sportster 900 — Duo Glide (1200cc)

1957 — XL Sportster 900

Key
Types of engine

Shovelhead (ohv)

1956

1955

1954 — KH (900cc)

1953

Panhead (ohv)

1952 — K (750cc) — X — Hydra Glide (1200cc) — X

1949

Knucklehead (ohv)

1948 — 74 (1200cc) — 61 (1000cc)

1944 — X

Flathead (sv)

1941 — 74 (1200cc) — 74 (1200cc)

1936 — 80 (1340cc) — 61 (1000cc)

ioe

1935 — 45 (750cc) — 74 (1200cc) — 61 (1000cc)

76

Continued from page 75

Continued from page 75

Continued from page 75

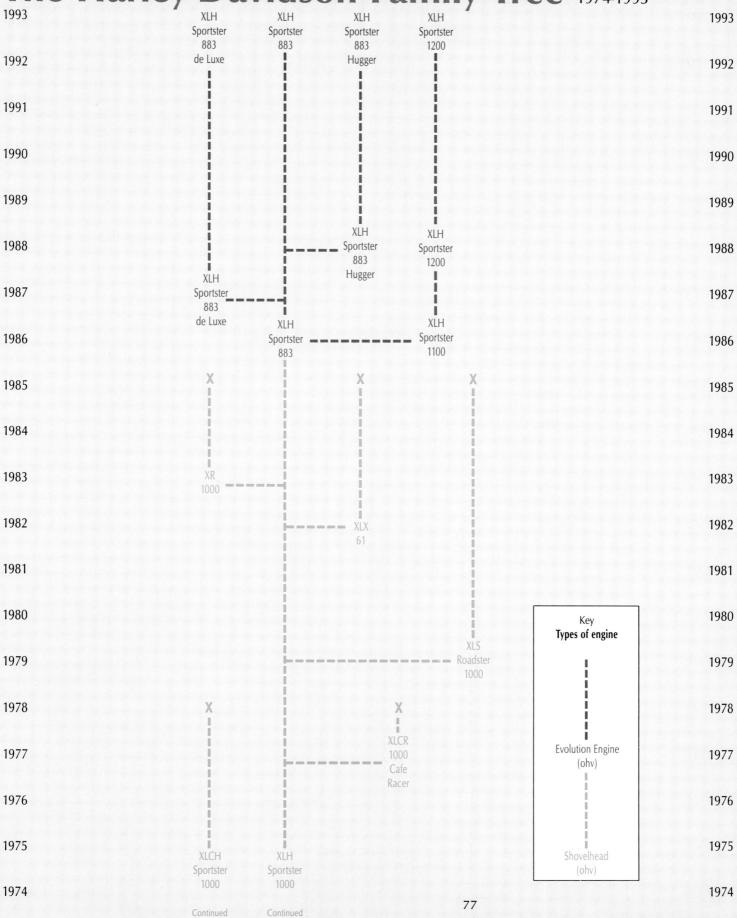

1993

XLH
Sportster
883
de Luxe

XLH
Sportster
883

XLH
Sportster
883
Hugger

XLH
Sportster
1200

1993

1992

1991

1990

1989

XLH
Sportster
883
Hugger

XLH
Sportster
1200

1988

XLH
Sportster
883
de Luxe

1987

XLH
Sportster
883

XLH
Sportster
1100

1986

X

X

X

1985

1984

XR
1000

1983

XLX
61

1982

1981

1980

XLS
Roadster
1000

1979

X

X

1978

XLCR
1000
Cafe
Racer

1977

1976

XLCH
Sportster
1000

XLH
Sportster
1000

1975

1974

Key
Types of engine

Evolution Engine
(ohv)

Shovelhead
(ohv)

77

Continued
from
page 76

Continued
from
page 76

**Key
Types of engine**

Evolution Engine
(ohv)
1340cc

Shovelhead
(ohv)

Year									
1993	FXLR Low Rider Custom	FXRS Low Rider Convert.	FXRS Low Rider	FXRS Low Rider Sport E.	FXDL Dyna Glide Low R.	FXDWG Dyna Wide Glide	FXR Super Glide	FXSTS Springer Softail	FXSTC Softail Custom
1992					FXDC Dyna Glide Custom	FXDB Dyna Glide Daytona	X		
1991						FXDB Dyna Glide Sturgis			
1990		FXRS Low Rider Convert.						X	
1989									
1988								FXSTS Springer Softail	
1987	FXLR Low Rider Custom								
1986			FXRS Low Rider Sport E.		FXRT Sport Gl. Grand Touring				FXSTC Softail Custom
1985	FXWG Wide Glide	FXEF Fat Bob	FXRS Low Rider				FXR Super Glide		
1984				FXRS Low Glide		FXRT Sport Glide		FXST Softail	X
1983			FXSB 80 Low Rider						
1982		X			FXRS 80 Super Glide II		FXR 80 Super Glide II	FXE 80 Super Glide	
1981									
1980	FXWG 80 Wide Glide	FXEF 80 Fat Bob	FXS 80 Low Rider	FXB 80 Sturgis					
1979	FXWG 1200 Wide Glide	FXEF 1200 Fat Bob							
1978			FXS 1200 Low Rider						X
1977									
1976									
1975								FXE 1200 Super Glide	FX 1200 Super Glide
1974									Continued from page 76

The Harley-Davidson Family Tree

FL series (Dresser)
1974-1993

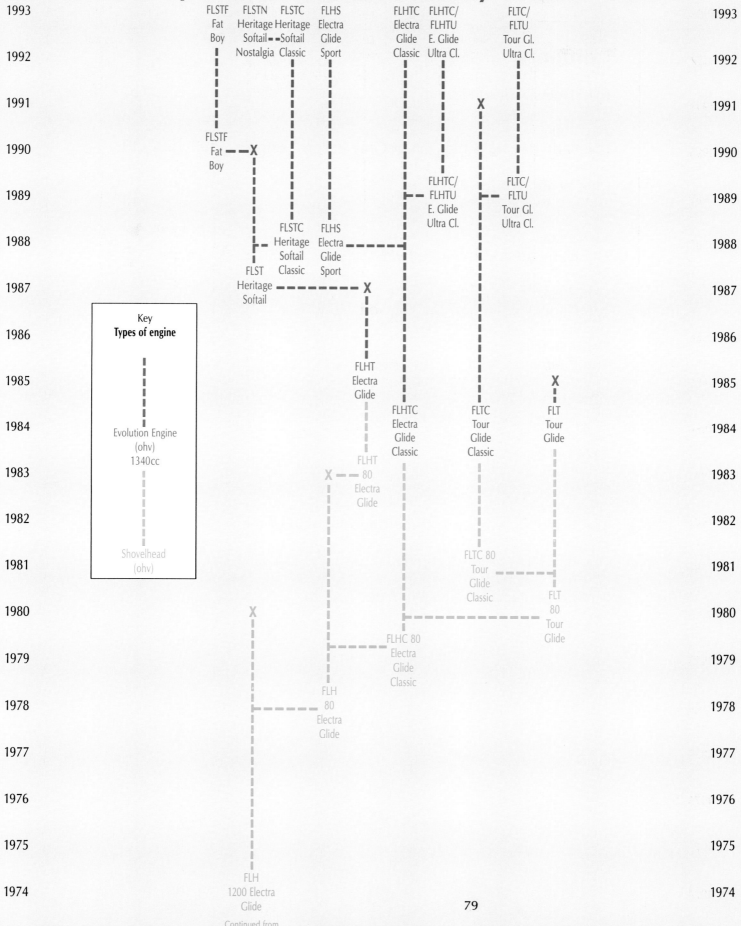

Key
Types of engine

Evolution Engine
(ohv)
1340cc

Shovelhead
(ohv)

1993 — FLSTF Fat Boy | FLSTN Heritage Softail Nostalgia | FLSTC Heritage Softail Classic | FLHS Electra Glide Sport | FLHTC Electra Glide Classic | FLHTC/ FLHTU E. Glide Ultra Cl. | FLTC/ FLTU Tour Gl. Ultra Cl.

1992

1991 — X

1990 — FLSTF Fat Boy — X

1989 — FLHTC/ FLHTU E. Glide Ultra Cl. | FLTC/ FLTU Tour Gl. Ultra Cl.

1988 — FLSTC Heritage Softail Classic | FLHS Electra Glide Sport

1987 — FLST Heritage Softail — X

1986

1985 — FLHT Electra Glide | X

1984 — FLHTC Electra Glide Classic | FLTC Tour Glide Classic | FLT Tour Glide

1983 — X — FLHT 80 Electra Glide

1982

1981 — FLTC 80 Tour Glide Classic

1980 — X — FLT 80 Tour Glide

1979 — FLHC 80 Electra Glide Classic

1978 — FLH 80 Electra Glide

1977

1976

1975

1974 — FLH 1200 Electra Glide

Continued from page 76

Contents

The Harley-Davidson legend 3

1901-1908:
The early days and the "Silent Gray Fellow" single 10

1909-1918:
The big twin and the First World War 18

1919-1934:
The Flathead and the little twin 26

1935-1945:
The Knucklehead and the Second World War 34

1946-1964:
The Panhead and the Sportster 40

1965-1973:
The Shovelhead and the first custom bikes 46

1974-1983:
Extending the range and starting again 52

After 1983:
The Evolution engine and the consolidation of the legend 62

The different types of engine 74

The Harley-Davidson Family Tree 75